# My Lifetime of Strange Coincidences and Weird Happenings

## BY FORREST CARR

How one ordinary person learned to experience precognition, visions, clairvoyance, lucid dreaming, and even miracles—and you can too.

# DEDICATION

For Deborah

# CONTENTS

# INTRODUCTION

Let me say right off the bat that I don't claim to have any special talent when it comes to phenomena that some might call paranormal or extrasensory. In fact, that's my entire point. I have come to believe that we all have at least some ability to sense or experience things that cannot quite be explained by taking into account the five senses we've all been told we have, or that can be laid out in fully logical detail by dry-eyed, rational scientists. It's my hope here to help you learn not only to tune yourself in to yours, but to be inspired to want to do so, and to embrace every moment life sends your way.

Once upon a time humans were much more prone to accept phenomena such as clairvoyance, second sight, precognition, visions, lucid dreams and even miracles unquestioningly. Of course, the problem is that superstitious humans of days gone by tended to see the work of God or the devil in just about *everything* that didn't immediately lend itself to rational explanation. As science and learning progressed, more lucid explanations began to fall into place. It became logical to assume that if science had not yet explained everything, it was only a matter of time before it would. The old world of gods, demons,

1

ghosts and sprites gave way to a new one ruled by rigid equations and solidly grounded natural principles. And the more science triumphed, the less fashionable it became to bring up things that didn't lend themselves so neatly to rational explanation. By and by we learned to shut up about such subjects, convincing ourselves that the paranormal and the occult were nothing more than devices for fun fiction.

Those who insist on talking seriously about bizarre and inexplicable phenomena tend to find themselves regarded as whackjobs and relegated to the fringe of society. The most persistent become the type of people who produce ghost hunting shows for cable TV. But there is a reason why so many viewers sit glued to the screen watching infrared video of guys and gals creeping around dark passageways shouting, "Hello? Is there anyone here? Give us a sign!" The reason is that in our heart of hearts, many if not most of us suspect that modern science really *doesn't* have a handle on every aspect of reality after all. We sense that something else is going on just outside the circle of scientific light.

And there is. One of the very few scientists to suggest that there is more to human experience than rationality can explain—and, having done so, survive with his reputation intact—was the famous psychiatrist Carl Jung, who followed in the footsteps of Sigmund Freud and built on his work. Jung got away with noticing the unnoticeable because he didn't try to explain any of it; he merely observed it. Simple observation is the very first step in the scientific method. But what absolutely must happen next for the scientific method to progress is not a step that you'll find written down any textbook. It's simply this: *accepting* what has been observed. History has shown time and again that scientists are quite willing to reject facts that don't fit their preconceived notions of reality and normality. Jung didn't do that. (We'll talk more about him later.)

Over the course of a lifetime, I have experienced a series of remarkable events that others might have chosen to simply ignore, events that may or may not have been paranormal in nature. Some of them have been what I'd call mind-blowing. A very small handful has risen to a level where one might even call them miraculous. The most common of these remarkable events involved premonitions—including one that led directly to this book, by way of putting me physically in a position to be able to write it. Had I not (1) experienced the premonition and (2) acted on it, time would have run out on me due to health issues before I could have even contemplated the project.

As remarkable as these events have been, they do not happen for me every day. In fact, they don't even happen every year. As I said, I claim no special ability. I believe that the realm of experiences I will talk about in the next few pages is similar to, say, singing: Most of us can do it at least a little, some can't carry a tune with a team of porters, and a small handful are born to be rock stars. I am no rock star. And that is my point. What makes me different from anyone else, to the extent that I am different, is that I have opened my mind over a lifetime and have simply observed. I've done so perhaps with a sense of wonder, but not with exaggeration. And I've documented. I took notes at the time of occurrence on many of the events I will relate here.

And most importantly of all, the happenings I will set forth have profoundly transformed my life.

Much of what you'll hear me talk about strikes me as unexplainable, at least in terms of the principles and natural laws that modern science recognizes. That said, I'm quite certain that skeptics could dispatch all of it within seconds. A lifetime of journalism has taught me to see all sides to a story, and I know the techniques skeptics tend to use. In any event, you will not hear me insist that any of the events I'll report to you are supernatural. I leave any such conclusions up to you. Nor are any such beliefs required in order for you to see the value and the meaning in the types of human experiences we'll discuss.

I do say that extreme skeptics tend to suffer from the same affliction as the extremely superstitious: Both sets of people proceed from false assumptions and operate under rigid belief systems that are not well suited to accept contravening facts. Unyielding skeptics insist that science and logic explain everything. The superstitious rely on spirits and alternate realities. I hope that in reading this book you'll walk a middle road and have an open mind. What's important is that you simply be willing to accept the facts, not to try to come up with explanations, although we will explore some of those.

Speaking personally, I do believe in science. But I also believe that human spirituality is quite powerful and that there are manifestations of it that lie outside the realm or understanding of traditional science. I do agree with the skeptics about this: All phenomena, even those that strike some people as paranormal in nature, must obey the laws of physics. If some events seem to transcend known scientific principles, then that can only mean there must be natural laws we have not yet discovered. Nor will they be as long as serious scientific inquiry remains closed to happenings that don't fit within currently accepted notions of reality.

I don't expect career scientists to suddenly remove their blinders. But perhaps I can persuade a few readers to remove theirs, and thereby open themselves to new vistas of human experience—and in the process, possibly gain new insight into those age-old questions about the meaning and purpose of life.

Before we proceed, let me tell you a bit about myself so you'll know where I'm coming from. I'm not some random piece of weirdness who sees UFOs around every corner, ghosts in every hallway, and monsters under every bed. I had a fairly distinguished 34 year career in broadcast journalism, about half of which I spent running various TV newsrooms. I won or shared credit in more than 90 professional awards, including some for investigative journalism. I'm the type of guy who, quite frankly, would not normally be prone to put his hard-won reputation on the line talking about the kinds of things you're going to read about in this memoir were it not for one very important circumstance: Cancer will kill me before very long, which sort of puts things into a new perspective for me in terms of my willingness to share these experiences. I claim no scientific credentials, only journalistic ones, and I have approached this work with that kind of serious attitude in mind.

Most of the anecdotes we'll discuss have one thing in common: They're personal in nature and entirely subjective. In presenting such testimony, I am by no means unique; Freud, Jung and many others also have relied extensively on personal experiences in their studies. The downside, of course, is that there is no objective witness who can verify what I did or did not dream and did or did not think prior to some of these events taking place. That, unfortunately, is one of the key factors that allow many (but not all) mainstream scientists to simply dismiss these kinds of human experiences out of hand as unverifiable and therefore insignificant. But they're wrong to do so. What has happened to me over a lifetime is in no way unique. The literature is filled with many, many other testimonies like mine. When you add it all up, strange coincidences and weird happenings like the ones I will relate here turn out to be a very basic part of the human experience.

And that is what I hope you'll take away from this book: the knowledge that there is more to our lives here on earth than meets the eye. I also hope you will come away with some inspiration, which will become clear as we proceed. You just have to open your mind and make sure you are not rejecting, even unconsciously, anything that doesn't seem to fit our modern society's accepted notions of reality. I'm convinced that almost anyone can experience the kind of events I will relate here, and does. If this book makes you a little more accepting of such phenomena, and a little bit more prone to talk about such things and even celebrate them, then my work here is done.

# 1 COINCIDENCES

I can go long periods of time and not ever encounter what one might call a "coincidence." But then suddenly there will be a flurry of them. Very seldom do any of them have any obvious meaning. But sometimes they do. 2013 was a banner year for them.

What do I mean by "coincidence?" Basically, in this context I'm referring to a random thought or a dream that doesn't seem to be significant at the time, but later turns out to coincide with a future event. Sometimes it coincides so dramatically with actual events down the road that the random thought, in retrospect, seems like it had to have been a premonition or foreshadowing. In the vast majority of cases, I am able to recognize such thoughts as a possible premonition *only* after the fact. Only rarely does a thought (1) present itself as a possible premonition at the time, and then (2) subsequently turn out to be true.

Here's a past example of what I mean by such a "coincidence"—in this case, it's a dream that didn't seem special at the time it occurred, but later turned out to have breath-taking significance. One night in 1999, I had a dream that I was scuba diving in jet black water, looking for gold aboard a sunken Japanese submarine. There was

7

absolutely no light, meaning that the wreck had to be in very deep water. In the dream, first I examined the bow, but that area was too damaged to permit entry. I started swimming along the hull toward the rear of the vessel, and then woke up. No big deal, and I really didn't dwell on it. I was left to wonder why I'd be dreaming about a sunken Japanese submarine—a subject to which I'd given zero thought during waking moments—but then again, strange dreams happen all the time, right? This one was quite vivid, but other than that it didn't seem to be any more significant than any other.

Later that morning while sitting in a doctor's office waiting room, I picked up a copy of *National Geographic Magazine*, thumbed through it, and then nearly fell out of the chair. There was my sub. It was the *I-52*, a Japanese submarine that was torpedoed[1] in 1944 about a thousand miles west of the Cape Verde Islands. The boat was on a mission to Germany, and among other things was carrying two tons of gold. The article, entitled "The Last Dive[2]," spoke about salvage operations. Unlike in my dream, no one was swimming around the sub, which lay in 5,000 meters of water, far too deep for any human to dive. But because of the depth, the water was inky black, exactly as in my dream. The bow area was damaged, as in the dream. There was a large hole in the hull, probably from a torpedo, aft of the conning tower, the direction in which I was swimming hoping to find an entrance when the dream ended.

When I saw this, I was absolutely floored. Coincidence? Skeptics would say, certainly. I'm not sure how even the most skeptical skeptic could explain how I just happened to have a dream so precisely matching the details of the wreck just hours before reading about it for the very first time. But, OK. Let's assume I'd heard earlier about the *I-52* in some other way and it had stuck in my subconscious mind even though I had no conscious recollection if it. That certainly sounds more reasonable than to suggest I had a paranormal experience. Doesn't it?

I will say that if the dream did contain any foreshadowing, it was not about the wreck, but rather about my *reading* about the wreck. And what makes that interesting is that while reading the article, I was sitting in the lobby of a medical clinic where I was about to undergo an endoscopic procedure that would require anesthesia. The procedure went fine, I'm happy to say. But as it turns out, this would not be the last time that one of these fascinating "coincidences" would be associated with medical trauma and anesthesia. In fact, during the year that is the subject of this chapter—2013—I would experience the mother of all premonitions, and it would revolve around medical procedures that involved multiple uses of anesthesia.

Call it what you will—coincidence, paranormal experience, precognition, heartburn, daydreaming, the vapors, the flibbityjibbits, whatever—of what practical value are "flashes" like the one I experienced regarding the *I-52*? Usually, no specific benefit ever becomes apparent, although in a moment I'll talk about some notable exceptions to that rule and also discuss the *general* value for such events. But in all cases, useful or not, these incidents are spooky as hell, and they tend to stick in the mind.

I was 13 years old when I first came to notice that something unusual might be going on with me. (Interestingly, this is the same general age often associated with poltergeist occurrences). That's when I started experiencing strange little coincidences and foreshadowings like the submarine vision described above, episodes where a dream or a random thought would enter my head that would later turn out to have an apparent connection with reality—sometimes, a quite dramatic one. In 99% of the cases, at the time such thoughts occur it's impossible to distinguish them right then and there as being potentially "meaningful." There's nothing obvious to set them apart from the thousands of other random thoughts, images and phrases that flit in and out of one's brain all day. Only in retrospect do they take on special significance. But such flashes have continued to occur every so often in my life since they began in my adolescence. Sometimes I can go years without a single one, and then something dramatic will happen.

Here's another example. In about the same period of time as the *I-52* dream, I had a dream about a friend whom I had not seen in about a decade, and with whom I had not spoken even by phone in some time. Because of the dream, I gave my friend a call. I then learned that he was going to be in a particular city traveling on business. Incredibly, I also was about to make a trip, and as it turned out, I would be in that very same city on the very same day. At the time, the two of us lived hundreds of miles apart, and our homes were hundreds of miles away from the city in question. To get there, I had to travel 2,000 miles east, and he had to go 850 miles southeast. But prior to my dream we had both made plans, independently of one another, to do just that. As a result of contacting him—which, remember, I did entirely because of the dream—we got to see each other for the first time in years. We rekindled our friendship and have kept in contact since.

An even more dramatic event took place about three years later. I stumbled out of bed one morning and, with my sleepy eyes half open, plodded down the driveway to get the morning paper. My groggy mind was still filled with images of the dream I'd been having just before the alarm had awakened me. The dream involved a helicopter crash. In fact, the last image that appeared in my dream, just before the alarm went off, was the front page of a newspaper with a headline proclaiming the crash, below which was a picture of the downed chopper.

With that dream image still on my mental computer screen, I bent down and picked up the newspaper. Focusing on it, I saw that across the top was a headline trumpeting a helicopter crash. Below the headline was a picture from the scene. It seems that the night before, a medical helicopter had gone down hard in an emergency landing, and only the quick actions of the pilot had saved everyone from disaster. The headline left me stunned.

But wait. There's more. About two hours later, shortly after I arrived at work, I got a call from an acquaintance of mine who lived on the opposite side of the continent. She'd heard something about a chopper crash in my city, and wanted to know if I knew anything about it. Boy, did I! The nature of her curiosity? Her former husband was locally employed as a medical helicopter pilot, and she was worried the crash might have involved his particular bird. I checked. Guess what? *It had.* It was his chopper that had gone down—and his quick actions that had saved everyone. I assured her he was OK.

But wait. *There's still more.* While she had me on the phone, she was curious to know whether I was acquainted with a certain person who had just applied for a job at her place of business (the three of us were working in TV news, but each of us lived in a different city.) Oh, yes, I knew the individual. He was a good friend of mine, and had worked with me in the same capacity. I gave him a stellar reference, and he later landed the job. He still works there today (and we remain good friends).

It was bizarre, and it was all connected to four people who themselves were interconnected. The incident's meaning, significance, and purpose, if it had any of those things, were not clear. But somehow, that crash had brought all four of us together—and my dream had foreshadowed the accident (or more precisely, the newspaper story about it) quite vividly.

Like many other of the incidents I'll relate here, this one was at least vaguely associated with a medical crisis. A couple of years after the dream and all that followed took place, I went to the hospital with a kidney stone. It was the most physically painful experience of my life, bar none.

I did not receive anesthesia, but the doctor did drug me into oblivion. The stone involved my left kidney. Hold that thought; the subject of my left kidney will come up again later in this narrative.

Only on very rare occasions have I recognized a random thought as a possible premonition at the time it occurred, and then the premonition subsequently turned out to be valid. Here are two examples, both of which served me very well. On both occasions, spaced years apart, I suddenly had a feeling that the vehicle driving in the lane directly next to mine was about to have a blowout. On both occasions, I dropped back. And on both occasions, the vehicle in question did immediately experience a blowout, and veered into the spot I had just vacated. In one of the two incidents, the car veered so violently that it continued on across the lane, smacked the guard rail, and spun out; I had pulled far enough back to avoid being hit, and subsequently was able to stop and render assistance (the driver was OK).

But, yes, to the skeptics I will admit that there have been at least two other occasions when I pulled back for similar reasons, only to watch the vehicle I was worried about sail serenely onward with no blowout. What's it all mean? I have no clue. Skeptics, I hear you. You're sure that it means nothing. I can't prove you're wrong. I'm not certain you are. But I remain intrigued. And the fact remains that had I not acted on the two premonitions that did matter, I could have been hurt.

Now that I've set the stage for the kind of event I'm talking about, let's circle back to 2013. This is where the story begins to get really, *really* interesting. For you to understand just how interesting, I have to lay out some background about how I chose my career, what that choice cost me, and what I felt I had left undone as this particular year approached.

For as long as I can remember, I've wanted to tell stories. My imagination has always been way oversized (and yes, I suppose you do get to take that into account as you read the events I'm laying out here). I remember at the age of 8 acting out scenes from the TV series *Lost in Space, Combat!, and Twelve O'Clock High*. My home's elevated back patio was perfect for the former. My best friend and I would set up lawn chairs at one end of it— those became the flight chairs for the Jupiter 2. A short set of steps at the left leading down to the yard, framed by iron guardrails, became the airlock. We even wore discarded Morton's salt cylinders on our backs as air tanks. I was the director, of course, and would lead us in all kinds of imaginary adventures.

I wrote my first short story in the 6th grade. It concerned an armed rebellion where the kids, operating flying desks complete with military armament, took over the school. This kind of prose would get you expelled today and probably thrust into intense psychotherapy. I'll leave it to the reader to decide whether my scribblings left me warped for life. But the record reflects that I have managed to avoid harming anyone or getting arrested for anything at all up to this point.

Some kids want to be firefighters or pilots when they grow up. I fantasized about being a science fiction writer like my lifelong idol, Robert Heinlein. I discovered, to my dismay, that breaking into that incredibly competitive field was not easy; there's no office to go where you can apply for such a job.

In college I studied broadcasting, because it struck me that it would be a lot of fun to go on the radio and be a smart aleck. And indeed, as it worked out my first job opportunity was in radio—just not on the entertainment end. Even before I graduated, I landed a full time but temporary job in the newsroom of WHBQ-AM, the radio station that bears the distinction of having introduced Elvis to the world. After a short time, the opportunity presented itself to work in the TV newsroom next door as a copy writer and a fill-in reporter. The gig seemed like a better idea than waiting tables while I worked on that first novel, so I took it. And, I figured I could always come back to radio if I wanted.

Fast forward to the end of 2012. By this time I'd risen up the ranks and had been working as a TV news director for about 15 years. I loved running TV newsrooms. However, the job is incredibly demanding. The news never stops, and a news professional is never truly off the clock. This doubly true if you're the guy or gal in charge. For me, any spare time for writing fiction had gone by the wayside years prior. I hated it—really, really hated it—but that's the way it was. I didn't give up the idea but I assumed that my dream of writing fiction would have to wait until retirement. I was just 55 years old. Retirement was quite a ways off.

The thing about planning for retirement is that in doing so, you're proceeding from an assumption that may not turn out to be valid—as life insurance companies' actuarial tables demonstrate in stark detail.

When the new year hit, that's when the premonitions began. A voice in my head began telling me, repeatedly, that my time was more limited than I'd previously thought. The voices became more and more urgent. A strong sense of foreboding settled on me, and I could not shake it. And I began to notice something: A lot of my colleagues in the business weren't making it to the finish line. TV news can be quite stressful, and company politics can make it even worse. This takes a toll. It's not uncommon to read about this person or that person in the business dying well short of retirement. In light of my forebodings, such incidents began to take on a new significance. The death of a news director in Alabama really shook me; I didn't know him, but the man collapsed at work (my nightmare scenario), and he was almost exactly my age. And then right after that a friend of mine who is a former TV news anchor died in his sleep. There were no warning signs; he simply didn't wake up. And he was about five years *younger* than I am.

Now very alarmed, I discussed my feelings with my wife. TV news can be a nomadic existence, and this is especially true for news directors, who, like college football and basketball coaches, are expected to show immediate dramatic results, and therefore tend to get hired and fired quickly. It may not be fair (it isn't) but that's the reality of the business. When the bride and I had moved to Tucson three and a half years earlier, we agreed that should I leave my job for any reason, rather than get another one like it right away—which would almost certainly require yet another in a long series of cross-country moves—I would try to find something in town in a related field, even though it would almost certainly involve a serious reduction in pay. Now, we amended the plan. I told her I would like to take a sabbatical of a year and a half or so, and use the time to begin writing my novels. We are fortunate in that both of us had worked in good jobs, and because we had no children we had been able to put aside some savings. She was very supportive and respectful, although as to what she felt about my early-death premonitions, you'd have to ask her. But I told her that should I wind up on my deathbed without having written the novels that have been bumping around in my head, I would die a bitter, pinched, miserable man. She believed it, and agreed to my plan.

I then did what they tell you never to do: I quit the day job in order to pursue my dream. This happened in March of 2013. I spent the next nine months writing and publishing two novels, and I started on a third. Let me tell you, I felt like I was in a race to make up for lost time, and I worked hard at it, writing for long hours every single day including weekends. But I had never been happier, even if I wasn't getting rich.

At the end of December I noticed an embarrassing symptom: Dull yellow-white globules of some kind began showing up in my urine. So I consulted a doctor. After undergoing a CT scan, one morning I got that phone call you read about and see in the movies: "Mr. Carr, I regret to inform you that you have a mass on your left kidney." A diagnosis of kidney *and* bladder cancer quickly followed. This led to two surgeries, from which it took me nearly three months to recover, and then I got back at it, resuming work on that third novel and also making a detour into talk radio, as I'd said 33 years earlier I might do some day.

Almost exactly two years to the day after I started my sabbatical—I had, in fact, already begun the process of trying to re-insert myself into the job market full time—the other shoe dropped. The kidney removal had not eradicated the cancer. I learned that not only do I have metastatic transitional cell carcinoma in the place where the kidney used to be, but that the same cancer had invaded my colon.

Of course, I'll get treatment and all that. But for me time will run out sooner rather than later. Even so, because I had acted on that premonition and changed my life accordingly, instead of being crushed at the news, I felt something akin to relief. If this had to happen, then thank God I had not waited another day to quit that TV news director job and chase my dream. And I do thank Him. Every single day.

In fact, for many years now I have embraced every sunrise. When I was 19 years old, I almost died—and certainly should have—mostly through my own stupidity. I have considered each day since that moment to be bonus play. I feel I have no gripes coming. The event that saved my life in 1976 might be called, by some, a miracle. We'll discuss that later. But it has left me predisposed to celebrate every moment, something I will continue to do even though I now know that my days are, perhaps, more numbered than for most of those who might be reading this right now.

As much as I have enjoyed all those "bonus days"—

and I have—news of my medical condition has filled me with a sense of absolute wonder. What if I had not listened to those premonitions in early 2013? In light of the diagnosis I would now consider my life to have been, at least in part, a blown opportunity. There's an old truism that when death approaches, no one will ever lament that they didn't spend more time in the office. Now that I'm at that point myself, I can assure you this is true. But I treasure every moment I've spent with friends and loved ones—and every stroke of the keyboard while working on my novels, blog and radio show.

Those 2013 premonitions caused me to make a major life change at the precise time it had to happen in order to allow me to accomplish my most-cherished and longest-nurtured unfulfilled life goals. Yet I had no way of knowing when those premonitions occurred that the deadline would be so tight. What made me pay attention? Don't we all have those little voices that whisper to us to do this thing or do that thing? What made me listen to mine?

But I know the answer to that question. I listened to my voices because a lifetime of experience has taught me to take premonitions seriously. I gave you several examples of the kinds of "flashes" and possible precognitions I'm talking about at the start of this chapter, and we will discuss more examples in the chapters ahead. At the time such events occurred, I had no idea what any of them actually meant. It all seemed so random! Now, however, the significance of all of these phenomena seems so much more clear to me. It is not hard for me to believe that the real purpose of that *entire lifetime* of "strange coincidences" was to soften me up and make me receptive to the one truly important premonition I'd ever have. Regardless of whether that was the "reason" for these earlier precognitive events, it certainly was the effect.

Skeptics, I hear you. "If anything, you have done nothing other than perhaps demonstrate above average personal insight and intuition." Maybe that is true. I agree no real conclusion is possible at this point.

But isn't it intriguing? We can debate all day about *why* these events took place, or whether there was even a "why" at all. But the *outcome* is beyond dispute. These perceptions did occur and they did change my life.

Before we dispose of 2013, there are several more incidents worth relating (as I said, it was a banner year). Three of them happened over the course of that year's Thanksgiving weekend—which in and of itself is remarkable, given that sometimes years can go by without a single noteworthy coincidence presenting itself to my attention.

First, during a break in working on my third novel, I spotted a headline on CNN.com proclaiming the then-approaching Comet ISON to be "The Zombie Comet." This really struck me, for two reasons. One, I had given ISON a major role in the sci-fi novel I'd just published (although in 2014 I downsized ISON's role when updating *A Journal of the Crazy Year* for the print edition, because the comet turned out to be a bust—as I had predicted in the original version of the novel, by the way). Interesting. Striking, even. But more than that, the novel contains a zombie plot (well, okay, they're not truly zombies in the novel, but they're similar enough to fit into the genre). Now here was a real news headline mentioning both my comet *and* directly associating it with the word "zombie." For me, ISON *already was* the "zombie comet" and had been so for some time! The coincidence was attention-getting, if not quite earth-shattering. Still, after catching up on the news, I shrugged it off and went back to work.

Which led to coincidence number two. My task on that day was to do some background research for a Scottish character I was thinking about writing into the plot of that third novel. I spent the afternoon researching Scottish culture, particularly idioms and drinking toasts. After a while, with visions of Glasgow pubs dancing in my head (a city that, trust me, I had never had any prior occasion to turn over in my mind or dwell on), I checked the news again. CNN.com had just posted a story about a helicopter crashing into a pub. Not just any pub. Wait for it: a *Glasgow* pub[3]. And for the second time that day, I found myself staring at the computer screen in open-mouthed astonishment.

Two nights later there was a third coincidence that had more personal significance. I had a dream about someone who was once very dear to me in my youth, but whom I haven't seen in many years. The circumstances of the dream made me wonder whether that person was OK. The dream was so vivid that I made a call to a mutual acquaintance to investigate. It was then I learned that the person in question was indeed experiencing a major medical crisis.

That was startling enough. As I said, this person and I were once very close. So to wake up thinking about this person for the first time in a while, be moved enough by that to reach out and check up, and then find out that my former friend was in health trouble was certainly remarkable. But what came later was even more amazing. Because of privacy concerns, I won't go into details about this person's medical condition. Suffice it to say that the dream was quite specific about a particular and somewhat unusual symptom this individual was suffering from. When I made the call, I found that although my former friend was very ill and had required hospitalization, the symptoms I was told about did not exactly coincide with what I'd seen in the dream. But six months later, a new symptom struck that did match what I'd seen in the dream—*precisely* so. That symptom has since come to define this individual's condition. The dream had progressed from having been precognitive to what some might call an actual vision.

But wait. I'm *still* not done with 2013.

Let's circle back to my novel, *A Journal of the Crazy Year.*

The purpose of it was to project into the future and explore this question: If current news trends continue, what might the future look like? By February of 2015—about a year and a half after initial publication—the novel was already shaping up to be prophetic enough to land me a guest shot on the famous radio program, "Coast to Coast AM." In particular, an incident in Memphis, where a mob of people descended on a grocery store parking lot and ran wild, knocking shoppers unconscious at random[4], was eerily similar to a scene in the book. And the disappearance of Malaysia Airlines Flight 370 bore a resemblance to a fictional scene from the book, where a pilot crashes an airliner on purpose for reasons that were entirely personal, not terroristic. Of course, the motives of the pilot or pilots on the Malaysia Airlines flight are not known and probably never will be. But it was damned spooky just the same. So I had a great conversation on national late night radio about, among other things, the strange parallels between what I had written and what was going on, and whether these events might be the precursors of a real-life Zombie Apocalypse (mine is based on an actual disease that, in theory, actually could return in a more virulent form as suggested in the novel).

Then less than a month after the interview, two incidents erupted during the same week that were, for me and my readers, nothing sort of mind-blowing.

First, there was the crash of Germanwings Flight 9525, which definitely *was* a case of a pilot deliberately crashing a plane in a bizarre act of mass murder/suicide. This real event was so close to the fictional scene in my novel that it sent a chill down my spine.

But a news story broke later that very same week that caused the hair on the back of my neck to stand up. A sleeping sickness had struck in Kazakhstan. News reports were referring to the affected town as "The Village that Fell Asleep[5]."

The reason this got my attention is that *A Journal of the*

*Crazy Year* is inspired by a real-life disease called *encephalitis lethargica*, which struck a century ago and caused its victims to lapse into a profound slumber from which most never awakened. A small number that did regain consciousness suffered from various psychoses including hyperviolence (that's the "zombie" angle). The pandemic disappeared without explanation and, for the most part, EL hasn't been seen since. Now here was a news story about a disorder that was causing some of the very same symptoms (although in what appears to be a milder form.)

Keep in mind the novel was already prophetic enough to warrant that radio show appearance *before* those two incidents. Oh, and did I mention, the novel has a comet making an historic close approach to the earth? In 2014 the comet Siding Spring made an historic close approach to *Mars*, closing to within a distance so tiny as to be without precedent in human history.

So, let's break this down, shall we?

Prediction: planet-brushing comet. Reality: check.

Prediction: violent flash mobs. Reality: check.

Prediction: murderous airline pilots. Reality: check.

Prediction: reappearance of sleeping sickness. Reality: check.

I don't assert that the novel is prophetic—yet. And I certainly don't claim that anything paranormal is involved. But my post about these coincidences zipped right to the top of my blog, out-pulling the average readership of all the other entries by a margin of more than 15 to 1. So I think we can agree that whatever else these coincidences might be, they're damned interesting.

As I said, 2013 was a banner year. In fact, it turned out to be the most important and powerful year I'd ever have for premonitions. But as fascinating at is was, when it comes to this type of phenomenon I have come to learn that I am in no way unique, and probably am not even that "talented" in this regard, if that's the right word. Through research, I've found that many millions of humans

21

experience such flashes and "feelings," especially about people that are close to them. For a handful of such individuals, the flashes occur quite often. And for many, the experiences are far more vivid and dramatic than anything that's happened to me personally. One of the definitive books on the subject of precognitive or extrasensory perception and communication is called *Phantasms of the Living*[6], and was written by researcher and psychologist Edmund Gurney all the way back in the 19th century. In fact, such incidents seem to be much more common to the human experience than ghost stories and poltergeist events, although the latter are what tend to get the most press.

My personal belief? I'm not sure that such experiences can be explained away as coincidental or as the products of an overactive imagination. I offer no proof. But I do have this suggestion: The human spirit is far more complicated, far more powerful, and far more interconnected than current science acknowledges. In fact, science does not recognize the spiritual side of humanity at all. Nor do the skeptics. Both would doubtless say that events of the type we've been discussing demonstrate nothing other than power of the human mind to delude itself. I know they'd say it because I've seen them dismiss on such grounds cases far more dramatic than anything I've experienced personally.

I can't prove them wrong. And they may not be. But it seems to me there are some things that we, as humans, simply don't know, and may never know. One is tempted to suspect that we aren't *allowed* to know about those things. We can't see what's behind the curtain. But it strikes me that we are at least allowed to know that there *is* a curtain, and that there *is* something behind it. And that is not nothing.

I've spent a lifetime pondering this. Next we'll discuss what got me thinking along these lines.

# 2 BORN WITH A SENSE OF WONDER

One night in May of last year (2014), for no particular reason I hauled out my late mother's photographs and began going over them. Contained in the collection is a set of school pictures of some of my first cousins, the daughters of my favorite uncle who passed away several years ago. I used to be quite fond of one particular cousin. But after she got married and moved out of her father's home, she exited my life, and we have not kept in contact. In the past 40 years, I've only spoken to her exactly one time, and then only briefly at her father's funeral. Now, going over those old photographs, I found myself looking at one of her taken when she was probably about 13 or so, exactly as I had remembered her. I thought about her fondly, and wondered how she was doing.

I got the answer to my question *the very next day*. She contacted me via Facebook. There was no reason. She was just thinking of me.

As it turned out, we were Facebook friends. Because I am an author, I often grant Facebook friend status to people I don't know, if we have some mutual acquaintances. Her current name meant nothing to me—she is using a first name other than the one I knew her by, and she's married. I had no idea who this person was until she contacted me—which she had not done *ever*. But she did do it on this particular occasion, which just happened to fall on the day after I spent several minutes remembering her with affection.

"Coincidences" like that never cease to amaze me (although by this point in my life, they've become, if not quite routine, at least not unheard of). I have, in fact, regarded the universe with a sense of wonder and amazement for as long as I can remember. And my recollection extends to a far earlier age than that of most people. It's said the average human can remember nothing before the age of about three and a half. Not me.

When I was very young, one night I looked out my bedroom window and saw lights dancing in the night. I was lying on my back at the time on a bed that had been secured with an add-on safety rail, having just graduated from a crib. This was before my sister was born, which means that I could only have been about two and a half years old. The lights were flying back and forth in front of my window, as naturally as a fish might swim in an aquarium. I looked more closely. Some of the lights had faces. One of them was quite ugly, like the visage of an old Halloween-style witch or hag. Even so, I didn't feel frightened, just enchanted. But I wanted to tell my mommy about it. So I crawled out of bed, went into my parents' bedroom, and climbed into bed with them. Motioning with my hands, I tried to describe what I had seen. Mom didn't understand what I was attempting to say, or even that I was trying to say anything. Hugging me close, she told me to go to sleep. I lay staring out the window for some time; the lights and faces were still there, milling about. Finally, I drifted off to sleep.

The next morning at breakfast, I really wanted to tell her what I had witnessed and ask her about it. My two and a half year old brain did not have the words. Frustrated, I looked around for something I could use as a comparison or demonstration. Out in the back yard stood a swing set and slide. The morning sun was glinting brightly off the latter's polished silver surface. I don't remember what sounds I made, but I distinctly recall pointing at the slide, and then waving my hands back and forth through the air, trying to get across the idea that the bright pinpoint of reflected sunlight was somewhat like the lights I'd seen moving outside my window the night before.

She didn't get it, of course. And I gave up. But that memory, and the wonder of that night, has stayed with me.

They say that young children are not able to distinguish between a dream and reality. I buy that. But still—what kind of dream is so powerful that it can happen at the age of two and a half and then stay with you *for life*?

You may doubt that anyone can remember anything, much less a dream, from such a young age. But I have even earlier memories, and am able to date at least one of them quite precisely. I recall distinctly the first time I ever pushed my father's lawnmower, and that as I did so, my mother (correctly believing that I was way cute) snapped a picture of me. The lawnmower engine was not running, of course. I had to raise my hands all the way over my head to reach the handles, which I quite clearly recall as being shaped like the handlebar grips of a tricycle, covered at the end with short white plastic sleeves molded to fit the fingers—although not mine, which were too small. The date stamped on the picture my mother took was June, 1959, making me 21 months old—and that assumes she had the film developed promptly, which actually is not likely, given that mother had a habit of sitting on negatives for a while before exposing the whole roll and then getting around to dropping them off to be processed. I can rule out that what I actually remember was pushing the lawnmower on some *later* occasion during which she also snapped a picture, because no such picture exists (we were not rich, and film was expensive. And my mother's entire photo collection is in my possession).

I have other impressions from the same age. I remember quite often that just as I was drifting off to sleep, I'd get a sensation of endless falling. It was by no means a terrifying feeling, such as falling off a ladder or a cliff would be. The sensation was pleasant—so pleasant, in fact, that I recall looking forward to it every night. On each occasion, I had the feeling of dropping endlessly through a colorless void. The nightly falling dreams only took place over a short period of time, and then I never had them again. The dreams disappeared before my sister was born (at which point I was 33 months old).

One might ask—and I have, many times since—how in the world would a toddler know what it feels like to fall endlessly? After all, a baby has never actually experienced any kind lengthy drop, because such an experience likely would be fatal. I didn't actually feel a sensation of weightlessness in *real* life even remotely like what I had felt in those dreams until the age of 15, when I soloed as a student pilot and was able to create such an effect for myself through flight maneuvers. Could the sensation that I felt as a very small child have been a reflection of some *other* kind of reality? And more to the point, how did my young, inexperienced brain come to associate the feeling of weightlessness with the concept of falling endlessly?

Let's hold that thought for a moment and fast-forward to something that happened when I was in the 4th grade. On the wall across from the foot of my bed was a small white plastic medallion, shaped with the points of a star, that I had received upon graduation from kindergarten. In the center was a classic pastoral scene showing Jesus the Good Shepherd tending a flock of sheep. One night something awakened me from a deep sleep, and I glanced over at the medallion. A shaft of moonlight was shining on the wall. Caught in the ghostly white beam where the medallion should have been was a grinning, evil-looking human skull.

What's a 4th grader to do in a situation like that? What would *you* do? What *I* did was to pull the covers over my head and lay there trembling with fright until the morning light.

It was many, many years before I told anybody about the incident. But what I did do at the time was to ask my parents to buy me a metal crucifix from the gift store at the Catholic Church we attended. My mother did that for me. Our parish priest blessed it, and then I hung the cross in place of the medallion. To this day, I still have both the cross and the medallion.

Let's accept, for a moment, that very young children can't distinguish between a dream and reality. To them, the lion under the bed is real. This psychological principle may be true, and probably is. But even if so, it doesn't appear to apply in all cases, even for toddlers. Perhaps when I saw lights "swimming" outside my window, it was just a dream, even though I thought it was real (and the memory of it seems real to this day). But also note that at about the same age, when I dreamed I was falling, I *knew* each experience was a dream, and in fact looked forward to sleeping so that I could feel it again. Even at the age of two and a half I didn't become confused and think I was *really* falling.

In any case, by the time you're 9, unless you're suffering from mental illness you absolutely *do* know the difference between a dream and waking reality. I don't know what happened the night I saw (or if you prefer, thought I saw) that ghostly skull, but I'm very certain I was *not* dreaming. You might choose to question my mental state, and I wouldn't blame you. But for the record, to date I have never been diagnosed with epilepsy, brain tumors or any kind of mental illness (except for teen depression, which we'll address later). Nor have I ever experienced any waking episode remotely similar to the one that night, which all these many years later still—well, "haunts me" would be too strong a phrase, but I've never forgotten it (in fact, the experience inspired a scene in my most recent novel, which I'm in the process of publishing as I type this).

Over the years I've only told the "skull" story to a handful of people. Recently, I learned that the wife of a friend of mine has had some training as a medium. I told her about the story. She thinks the possibility exists that I was subjected that night to some kind of spiritual attack.

Now here's where the story gets creepy again. Two nights after typing the sentence above, I saw the skull again for the first time in nearly five decades. No, this time there was no doubt about whether I was dreaming. Quite definitely, I was having a nightmare (in fact, it was a sleep-paralysis nightmare, a type we'll discuss in more detail later). But in the dream, I opened my eyes, beheld that skull on the opposite wall, and was absolutely transfixed in bed, unable to move. The skull opened its mouth as if to speak—and I screamed. Folks, only on the rarest of occasions do I ever have nightmares, and I cannot recall a single instance of *ever* having bolted straight up in bed and awakened myself screaming on any prior occasion in my entire life.

It's no great leap of the imagination to suggest that I had this nightmare because I'd dwelled, for the purposes of this narrative, on that old incident from many years ago. And even though that previous event struck me as not a dream, but rather as something that had happened while I was awake, who knows? Maybe my 4th-grade vision of that skull was nothing more than a really bad, very realistic nightmare after all. Whatever it was or was not, research has shown me that my experiences are in no way unique. As it turns out, spooky incidents of this type—and in this case, now I'm talking about events that may or may not involve other entities or at least the suspected perception of them—are quite common to the human experience. And they happen to some people more than others. There's a name for folks, in fact, who have many such experiences over the course of a lifetime. No, not whackjobs. Mediums.

I stand mute about whether I might be one of the former, and I make no claims regarding the latter. But I do wonder ("suspect" would be too strong a word) whether very young children might be more susceptible to experiencing certain kinds of phenomena that most adults can't see. More to the point—could those lights outside my window have been something other than a dream—perhaps even a child's eye view of some kind of spiritual encounter? Might my friend have been right about that skull on the wall being the result of a spiritual attack? If so, might the entity responsible for the attack still have its eye on me all these years later? Could that childhood "falling" dream have had a correlation to something real—something that I was experiencing, or had experienced in the past, regarding the travels of *my* spirit?

Well, I don't claim any of those things is true. But it sure does add to my life-long sense of wonder and amazement at the universe.

After my mother hung that crucifix on the wall, nothing else out of the ordinary happened for a long time. The next incident that might fairly be labeled "spooky" or something like it occurred when I was about 14 or 15. Throughout my childhood, my family kept at least one cat, usually two. One night as I was drifting off to sleep, I felt the bed bounce lightly. I could tell that the cat visiting me was not my buddy Cruford, our Siamese male who regarded me as his person. That meant it had to be TC, a female calico who didn't claim anyone as a person, and who consequently visited me much less often. I knew this because of the way the bedsprings bounced; TC (which stood for "Top Cat") was much lighter than Cruford. I didn't like for TC to be in the room, because she had a habit of visiting only for a short while, and then scratching at the door to get out, which caused me to have to drag myself out of bed just as I was drifting off to sleep. So normally every night I did a room check before shutting the door and turning off the light, in order to make sure I hadn't shut her in with me. *I must have missed her*, I thought. *Sneaky little thing.*

After a while, the bed bounced again as she jumped down. I moved my foot over the vacant spot where she'd been lying, and at this point I realized that I'd better get up and let her out now before I'd fallen fully asleep, or else she'd wake me later from a profound slumber, which would be even more annoying. I got up and went over to the door.

She wasn't there. Turning on the light, I looked around the room. Nothing was in sight. I checked under the bed and then poked into the closet. Nothing. There was no cat in the room.

I was a little weirded out. But I didn't know what else to think other than that I'd probably imagined it. Certainly there wasn't a thing to do about it other than to hope I wasn't losing my mind. I shrugged it off and went back to bed. And I didn't think about it again—until the next morning at the breakfast table, when my mother said, "The strangest thing happened last night."

*She then related a story about a phantom cat visiting her in bed.*

Now I was *totally* freaked out. For the next several nights, I will admit that sleep didn't come easily. You might be curious to know whether we suspected that we knew the identity of the phantom cat. Yes, we'd had a kitten that had disappeared about five years earlier. But no one had the courage to say the name out loud. Regardless, whatever had happened, it never happened again, to any of us.

Still, those were not the last strange occurrences during that period of time. In fact, the fun was just beginning, although what started to happen next was a completely different type of phenomenon. In about my freshman year of high school, I began to hear the alarm clock go off seconds before it actually did. I don't mean that I would wake up and open my eyes just before the alarm sounded. I mean that in my mind I would hear a "click" as the alarm tripped, followed by a song as the radio circuits came to life. I did not mistake this mental sound and the music that followed as being *real*; I knew it was only in my head. But it did wake me up. And then invariably, just seconds later, the alarm would actually go off with a loud click, and then the song actually coming out of the radio speaker would be the same one already playing in my mind.

At this point, skeptics will be able to chalk up absolutely everything I've said to dreams, half-asleep twilight fantasies, and coincidence. As noted, the former require one to believe that even a 9 year old can't discern reality from a dream, but I've read enough in the years since to know that even some adults actually do have that problem. I don't think I do, but fine. As for the latter, certainly it's not unusual for a person's body clock to go off, especially if one wakes at the same time every day. And if the radio is set to a Top 40 station, how many song choices can there be, anyway? You're bound to hit one sooner or later that was already playing in your brain, and when you do, *boom*, it screams "precognition" when really it's just a coincidence.

I get those arguments. But keep in mind that the alarm clock phenom happened to me not once, not twice, but time after time after time. On one occasion the song that played in my head just before the alarm went off was an obscure Uriah Heep tune that I'd never even previously heard played over the radio, and have not heard since (I was familiar with the song only because I had the album). On several occasions I woke up, opened my eyes, and actually pointed my finger at the radio, only to have it click and start playing a split second later with the song I was already hearing in my brain. Random chance does not explain it, in my view, or at least doesn't explain all of it.

I admit I can prove nothing. But here's where the "it's just coincidence" theory falls very short. Throughout my entire life, I have used a clock radio and have always had it set to awaken me with music. I always choose a pop music station. And, just like in my school days, every weekday I always wake up at the same time. But my ability to open my eyes just seconds before the clock goes off, and to predict the song I am about to hear by way of having it play in my head before the radio actually switches on, ended utterly early in my Junior year of high school and never returned, having lasted for a period of about a year and a half. If this truly had been nothing but coincidence, shouldn't I still be having this experience today?

My trick with the alarm clock was intriguing. But a few months after that started happening, I had my first real precognitive dream. I hesitate to use the word "vision," but it certainly was visual. And it blew my socks off.

At this point in my life, I was training to become a private pilot. I had soloed in a Piper Cub. Basically, that model of plane is a kite with an attitude, a huge wirelike frame covered with coated fabric—in this case, bright orange fabric—and fitted with an engine. After flying the Cub for a while, I graduated to a Cessna 150. Just north of the airport was a huge dirt lot that had just been bulldozed for a warehouse complex. One night I dreamed I was flying over it in the Cessna. Looking down, I saw that the bright orange Cub that the flying club owned had landed on a rough dirt lane that had been dozed in the orange soil—a lane that was destined to be a road or a driveway once the project was complete. This seemed unusual to me, because the spot where the plane had landed was only about a mile from the airport. Why would someone land there? Then the dream ended. I gave it no more thought. The next day I went flying in the Cessna for real. On the return approach to the airport, I flew over the development. I looked down—and have you guessed yet what I saw? There was the Cub, parked on the dirt lane in all of its radiant bright orange glory *exactly* as I had seen in my dream.

When I beheld this, I am not kidding when I say that an electric jolt passed down my spine. I felt like I really had glimpsed the future the night before. This gave me a weird, haunted feeling that it took me a week to shake. As it turned out, it was a feeling I'd have again. And by the way, upon my return I learned that the Cub had landed there because of an in-flight emergency. A gasket had failed, dumping hot engine oil onto the legs and feet of the pilot, who was a friend of mine. He suffered some burns, and was very lucky he wasn't killed trying to get the plane down.

The experience left me a little unnerved, but also fascinated. Other incidents like it began to happen, although nothing so dramatic. A name would pop into my head for no reason, and then I'd see the same name in the paper or hear it on television. The radio song precognitions continued to occur with great regularity, and so on. There were enough of these noteworthy occurrences that I began to keep a tape-recorded journal (which, alas, I have since lost).

Eventually—perhaps as my hormones settled down with adolescence—the pace of new incidents began to drop off. The radio precognitions slowed and then stopped altogether. And as I entered college, I more or less forgot about all of it.

Then ten years later, in 1985, three incidents happened in quick succession that rekindled my interest in the whole thing.

# 3 THE FLASHES RESUME

By the age of 27 or so, I had pretty much put behind me the unusual coincidences and other strange happenings that had taken place earlier in my life. I was now a level-headed news professional, employed in a big city TV newsroom and not appearing to be any more of a loon than anyone else working in that kind of environment. But then three incidents happened in rapid succession that made me sit up and say, "Wow." All three were spectacular. At the time, only two of them struck me as significant, but in retrospect, all three were. Each was breathtaking in its own way.

The year was 1985. I was working as a newscast producer at a TV station in Texas. In every such newsroom, managers and others gather daily in the morning editorial meeting to choose stories and divvy them up by newscast. Sometimes the available selections are pretty lame. On such occasions our boss, whom we'll call Marla, would sigh and say, "It's time to pray for spot news." Spot news basically consists of an important but unplanned and unforeseeable incident that erupts without warning "on the spot." For local newsrooms, such stories most often first present themselves by way of the police and fire scanners, which are installed on the assignment desk for the purpose of eavesdropping on official radio transmissions. Take it from me: Nothing good for humanity ever comes over police and fire scanners.

Marla's statement that she would pray for spot news is something she'd said many times before on many other dull coverage days. Nor was she the first colleague I'd ever heard utter such a prayer. But for some reason, I chose this particular morning to raise an objection.

"Marla, don't pray for spot news," I said. "You're asking for mayhem. Those prayers don't go up. They do down. It's a form of devil worship."

She laughed off the comment. But as I recall, I persisted, urging her to retract the prayer, while pointing out that nothing but tragedy ever results from any plea for spot news.

I can pinpoint the date for this verbal exchange with precision—not because I remember the year, month and day so clearly, but because I can look it up. It was August 2, 1985. In mid afternoon later that day, Delta Flight 191 crashed while attempting to land in a thunderstorm at Dallas-Fort Worth International Airport, killing 137 people. It was the lead story on all of our newscasts that day, of course, and for many days afterwards.

Marla's prayer for spot news had been answered. She was quite shaken up about it, and vowed never to pray for spot news again.

The significance for me, of course, is that for the first time in my life, I had warned of a possible tragedy, urged corrective action, had been ignored, and then watched as a disaster unfolded. I had not, of course, in any way predicted the nature of the tragedy. But still—it struck me as quite remarkable.

A short time later a second, similar incident occurred—only this time, it didn't seem so serious. In fact, it was hysterically funny, and prompted a round of laughs all round. The true meaning of it didn't strike me until much later.

As has been the case for the other anecdotes in this book, the details for the story I'm about to relate are true and are not exaggerated in any way. The dialogue is approximated from memory but reflects the spirit of what was said. I have changed the names so as not to embarrass anyone.

My daily job assignment during this period of time was to put together each day's 6 pm news broadcast. The producer is the person who makes most of the decisions about the newscast, arranges the stories, and writes most of the anchor copy. The 5 pm producer, whose name was not Leslie, was a friend of mine, but also a rival. Management in that shop considered her newscast to be more important than mine; my 6 pm news program was the red-headed stepchild. What this meant in practical terms is that in the daily editorial meetings our boss, the aforementioned Marla, usually handed Leslie most of the really good stories. My newscast had to make do with the leftovers that Leslie didn't want or couldn't fit in.

One morning, Leslie passed up a story that had great potential, but which had not yet been shot. It concerned allegations that rats were overrunning a downtown sandwich shop, and that in the morning hours the rodents could be plainly seen through the restaurant window having a grand old time. Now, the thing to know about story assignments of this nature is that it was risky for a producer to accept one and then count on having it for that day's newscast, given that the event being covered may or may not actually happen. If, as producer, you were to select such a story as your lead, you could wind up with nothing. But the idea of potentially getting video of rats overrunning the restaurant was too juicy for me to pass up. Leslie, having been burned before when spec stories cratered, was only too happy to let me have it. She assumed, in fact, that I'd wind up with nothing and have to start my news program with something lackluster, like a city council meeting or some such.

But when the video came back later that day, it exceeded our wildest expectations. The rats were having a party and absolutely everyone was invited. The pictures were quite stunning—rats on the restaurant floor, rats on the counter, rats in the mixing bowls. *Ewwwwww.* Leslie grumbled, but a deal was a deal.

Except that it wasn't. By mid afternoon our supervisor, Marla, had figured out what was going on. She took the story out of my newscast and gave it to Leslie without apology. Yes, life is not fair.

Leslie thought she'd pulled one over on me, and was very smug about it. "My newscast is going to kick your butt," she assured me.

Now, I'm not saying I'm superstitious, but I'd been raised not to tempt fate with braggadocious comments predicting the success of a project or endeavor in advance of the fact. I pointed out to Leslie the danger of doing such a thing, and added, "You'd better knock on wood," which my mother had told me was the remedy when one had blurted out such comments unthinkingly. But Leslie scoffed at this idea.

It then occurred to me that not only had Leslie tempted fate in a very dangerous and provocative way, but that she'd picked the worst possible day on which to do so. "Leslie, this is Friday the 13th," I pointed out. "Really. You need to retract the comment, and knock on wood."

She looked at me with an expression of utter contempt. "Oh, give me a break," she said, rolling her eyes. "This newscast is going to wipe the floor with yours, and there's not a thing you can do about it. Quit your whining."

I shrugged. "It's your funeral," I said with as grim a tone as I could muster. "But mark my words, you are going to regret what you said."

Now, let me interject at this point that I am not what you would call a superstitious person per se. But on the other hand, who among us is so knowledgeable that we can claim to know absolutely everything about how the universe works? The salient point here is that for whatever reason, I had a very strong feeling that really bad things were about to happen to Leslie's newscast.

Two and a half hours later, the editors had prepared the video tapes and stacked them for playback, all scripts were in place, and the carefully coiffed anchors were sitting on the set, ready to go. The open to the newscast rolled. A tally light blinked red on one of the studio cameras. The anchors gave their customary greeting, and then the male anchor began to read the intro for the rat story. At that precise moment, an overhead studio light above the anchor ruptured.

Now, studio lights do burn out from time to time, often with a flash and an audible *pop*. This was nothing like that. The lamp exploded as if someone had placed a cherry bomb inside it, sending flaming shards of glass and smoking bits of red hot metal flying through the air and showering onto the anchor desk. A few pieces landed on the anchor's head and shoulders. Pandemonium erupted as he brushed wildly at his head and clothes, and the floor crew rushed to help him, all of which unfolded live on the air. The acrid odor of burning hair drifted through the studio.

Within a few moments, everyone had settled down. The anchor gracefully apologized, and then started the lead-in from the beginning, concluding with, "Reporter Jane Sittenfijit has that story," which was the director's cue to roll the tape. But instead of the promised video of rats mobbing the restaurant like Beatles fans at Shea Stadium, what viewers at home saw was the picture flip and then go to snow. Simultaneously, every light in the studio went dark.

There had been a power failure. And since the TV station had no emergency generator, there was nothing anyone could do but wait for the power company to restore the juice. Repair crews did so about 20 minutes later. But the damage had been done. The blackout had completely trashed the newscast. Later we learned that a blown transformer at a nearby substation had been the culprit. And get this: The outage had affected only a handful of buildings within a small radius of our TV station. It was almost as if our studio had been the target.

The 5 pm newscast having crashed and literally burned, the rat story wound up in my program after all, which then proceeded to air flawlessly. Afterwards, Leslie refused to accept that the events were the result of any tempting of fate on her part by her failure to knock on any wood. Truly, I didn't believe they were, either. But the true significance of what had transpired didn't occur to me until many years later, when I began compiling my personal list of strange happenings.

And here it is: As it turns out, this was the second occasion where I predicted a mishap out loud, advised someone to take corrective action, was ignored, and then got to stand by and watch the disaster I'd warned about unfold before everyone's eyes. Of course, in this case the "disaster" in question was only a ruined newscast. But it was no less dramatic.

For my next act, I would utter words describing a mishap in precise detail, and then watch it happen exactly as stated. And I mean, *exactly*.

By about a year later (my memory of the date is approximate) my work shift had been changed to the late news. Marla had a habit of issuing continual reminders to me before leaving at the end of her day. And sometimes, when she got home, she'd call me again with additional reminders. On one evening, she'd come by my desk more times than usual with admonitions not to forget this and not to forget that for the 10 pm broadcast. After the last such reminder, I exclaimed, "Marla, go home! And *don't* call me when you get there! I don't want to hear from you again tonight unless it's to tell me that you've just looked out your window and spotted a four-alarm fire!"

Laughing, she assured me that she would not call me unless such a thing were to occur.

90 minutes later, my phone rang. It was she. "Marla," I said, exasperated, "What did I tell you? You weren't supposed to call me short of a four-alarm fire burning within view of your apartment."

"Forrest," she said, deadly serious. "That's why I'm calling. The building across the street is burning down. I can see it from my window."

The fire was my lead story that night. It went to four alarms.

As I mentioned earlier, for me weird coincidences like this often happen in clumps, usually after long dry spells. Those three were the most dramatic I'd had in about a dozen years, and they rekindled my interest in the general phenomenon.

Some such incidents in my life have been associated with health issues. These were not, at least not in any way that I could tell. And after the last one mentioned above, there wouldn't be another for about four years. But it was very memorable.

I had a dream one night that I had picked up the morning paper to read that a well known cultural institute in my city was having a funding crisis. The image was so powerful that when I got to work, I double checked the morning and afternoon papers and also the news wires to see if any such story had crossed in recent days. Nothing. Two mornings later, when I went to pick up the paper, there it was, with the headline exactly as I had seen it. This was the first time I had "flashed" in advance onto something in print that I had not yet actually read, and it left quite an impression. But as we saw in the previous installments in this series, it would not be the last. The best was yet to come.

# 4 MY MOST MIND-BLOWING COINCIDENCES

After the premonitions and flashes I experienced in Texas, there followed another very long dry spell. For me, this in no way unusual. But even the dry spell was interesting. During this time, minor little events did continue to present themselves to me from time to time. Mainly those took the form of incidents where a word, name, phrase, or image would pop into my head and stay there, leaving me to wonder why this thought or that thought had suddenly occurred to me—and then a short time later, I would read it in a book, magazine, or newspaper, see it on television, or have someone bring it up in conversation.

Here is an example of what I mean. This incident is from much later, but I happened to record it in my notes, and it's indicative the kind of thing I'm talking about. One afternoon, for no apparent reason, the name "Sonja" popped into my head—Sonja with a "J." I didn't know anyone named Sonja. I gnawed on it off and on all day, wondering what had propelled this unusual name into my consciousness. The next day, I picked up the morning paper, and there it was, in an above-the-fold story. Sonja was the first name of one of Danny Rolling's 8 serial murder victims, for which he had just gone on trial. Skeptics will argue that, being in the news business, undoubtedly I'd heard the name before and had simply forgotten about it, until one day when it bubbled back up from my subconscious mind. Okay. I won't argue. Maybe so.

Here's another example of what I'd call a "minor" flash of that type, recorded at about the same time. I had a dream that I was in a house where some kind of party was going on. Someone brought in large cat, the size of a Florida panther or a cougar. The cat was going from person to person, jumping into people's laps, etc. In the next day's paper was the following headline: "Girl, 4, mauled by captive cougar at birthday party."

Aside from minor incidents of that nature, which have occurred every so often throughout my life since about the age of 13, nothing else major happened until I was about to turn 45. By this point in my career, I was a large-market TV news director. Nearly every year I would attend the annual Radio-Television News Directors Association convention. But as I began to make plans for the upcoming event, I started to experience a feeling of foreboding, bordering on dread. Every time I thought of the convention dates, a pervasive sense that something really awful was about to happen weighed down on me. The feeling of dread was quite oppressive, and I couldn't shake it. I had no idea what the incident might turn out to be, but I felt it would be massive, a major news event with national ramifications that would preclude me from attending the convention. I was so convinced that something along those lines would occur that I put off making travel plans. Finally, as the deadline loomed, having no rational reason to do otherwise I went ahead and booked my flights. But my forebodings were so strong that I did something I had never done before, and have not done since. Even though it was more expensive,

I bought fully refundable airline tickets. Somehow, I just *knew* I'd be collecting that refund.

My scheduled date of departure: September 12, 2001.

I'm sure I need not tell you what happened or why I never took that flight. On my departure date, the only aircraft flying in the country were military jets. The news convention had to be canceled. I don't know if I was the only news director in America to have bought a refundable ticket for that event. But if there were any others, I'd bet long odds there were damned few, and that none did so for the same reason I had.

And by the way, here is an interesting postscript that may raise an eyebrow for you; it certainly had that effect on me. The latest personal coincidence connected with that canceled convention came to my attention *just this very minute*. Just before typing this paragraph, I did a quick Internet check to confirm my recollection that the RTNDA convention had been scheduled to start on 9/12 of that year. A article popped right up[7] from an author recounting his experiences on the morning of 9/11, detailing exactly what happened to those who'd already arrived for the convention and how they dealt with what was going on. I was surprised to note that the posting date of the article was *just two nights ago*, relative to the time I am typing this. I began outlining this chapter in my mind— guess when?— *two nights ago*. The article was a reprint, which the RTDNA (as it's now called) website had just reposted. There was no obvious reason for the timing of the repost, and none was given. This year's 9/11 anniversary is still more several months away as I compose this. But the article reappeared on line at the exact time I needed it to do so.

Interesting, is it not?

Now on to what, until my premonitions about my health, had been the most breathtaking of all the coincidences I've experienced. This one involves not just me but my wife. In fact, I'm not sure whether it directly involves *me* or not at all, given that it started with *her* dream.

In early 2008, because of a death in the family my wife Deborah and I had to make a trip to San Diego. On the morning of the funeral, Deborah woke up and said she'd been having a dream about the rock band America. Deborah very rarely mentions her dreams to me. Why she would feel compelled to tell me about this one, I don't know. But apparently it had been a pleasant dream. The band had been playing one of her favorite songs.

Later that morning when we got into my sister Amy's car, Amy popped in her iPod, and what do you think would come out of the speakers but an America tune—the very one, in fact, about which Deborah had been dreaming. The coincidence was remarkable, if just barely. But it did cause Deborah to mention her dream. And then we chatted a bit about the band. America is one of our favorite groups, and previously Deborah and I both had a chance to meet them during a concert in Tucson, by virtue of the fact that Deborah worked for the concert venue at the time and had helped promote the band's appearance. In fact, she'd met them on *two* occasions, to my one. In the course of discussing all this, I checked my sister's iPod and noticed that she'd happened to play the one and only America song she owned, which was just one of several hundred tunes on the device. This was, in and of itself, not amazing—just interesting. And it was not something I would have remembered, if not for what was about to take place.

The next day, we flew back to Fort Myers. The airline lost our reservation, and to make up for it agents wound up sticking us in first class at no extra cost, to which we raised nary an objection. On the second leg of the flight, I couldn't help but notice that the two people sitting behind us were talking in terms that made me suspect they were roadies for a rock band.

Can you guess what's coming? I turned around.

There, just two seats back, sat Gerry Beckley and Dewey Bunnell, two of the three original members of the band. America was on the plane with us, on the way to a concert in south Florida.

After we landed, my wife and I couldn't help ourselves. We approached the two of them at the baggage belt and introduced ourselves. Both guys remembered Deborah. We explained the strange coincidence. They were quite nice about it, and then as soon as they politely could, they beat it out of there, moving as fast as their feet could take them without actually breaking into a trot.

So what are the odds of all those things lining up at once? To recap, the sequence was as follows:

(1) A dream about America, which led to:

(2) A conversation about America.

(3) An America tune being selected out of hundreds for playback, which led to:

(4) Another conversation about America.

(5) A lost reservation, leading to:

(6) A first class seating assignment placing us two rows ahead of America, a band that just happened to be on the same plane, which led to:

(7) My wife discussing her dream about America *with* America.

I tried to figure the odds for this, and came up with a figure of something like 1 in 30 quadrillion. (Some of the values that went into the calculation were fairly arbitrary, though. For instance, how do you calculate the odds that someone will have a dream about a particular thing on a particular night? I used a number of 1 out of 365. Since she'd never had such a dream before, I could just as easily have divided by the total number of days so far in Deborah's life, as opposed to the days over the past year, which would have produced even longer odds.) Such an improbable event seems impossible. But then again, so does winning the lottery, yet it happens all the time. In fact, it's been said that stating any probability less than zero is just another way of saying that something *will* happen, sooner or later. And after all, the band members had to sit next to someone.

But, still. I mean, sheesh!

Only one other thing happened in this period of time of any note, but it also was a stunner.

The year after the above incident, I moved to Albuquerque to run a TV newsroom there. One day soon after my arrival an incident happened of the kind where a name pops into my head for no apparent reason. In this case, it was the name and face of a reporter acquaintance of mine whom I had not seen in more than 15 years. Idly, I wondered why the thought of this person, whom we'll call Kathi, would suddenly appear on my mental radar. I might not have given it much thought, except that now that I was thinking about her, I couldn't remember her last name to save my life (it sucks to get old). I gnawed on it for a while, and finally recalled it.

About two hours later, an email appeared in my mailbox from this very person. The subject line read, "What the hell?" My first impression, instantly rejected, was that Kathi somehow had known I was thinking about her and was now demanding to know where I had gotten off doing that. Upon opening the email, I saw that Kathi had just heard about my new job, had seen that I had moved to her region of the country, and was wanting to catch up.

Now, keep in mind that *I* didn't know I *had* moved to her region of the country. When I knew her, we both worked at the same station in Texas. In the intervening years, we had communicated maybe twice via email, and not at all in the last nine years. We'd been friendly acquaintances but not particularly close. I'd completely lost track of her and had even not thought of her more than once or twice in years.

So. Would you care to guess where Kathi now was? Did you guess "Albuquerque?"

Sorry, that's too obvious. Let's see if you can narrow it down. What do you think was the physical distance between me and Kathi at the moment her name popped into my head, and when she fired off that email?

Go ahead. Venture a guess. I'll wait.

At that very moment Kathi was 150 feet away. She was at a desk in a building *on the other side of the street.* And it was a narrow street. Kathi was employed at a competing TV station which happened to be located in the same plaza as mine. It's where she'd been sitting when I had, for no apparent reason, thought of her, not knowing whether she was within a thousand miles of me. And it's where she'd been sitting when she popped off an email, almost as if in answer to my thought.

"What the hell" indeed.

# 5 WEIRD COINCIDENCES, STRANGE HAPPENINGS, BALL LIGHTNING, AND YOU

At the age of 57, I can look back on numerous weird mental flashes and bizarre coincidences that have taken place in my life, of which a handful (but *only* a handful) were truly spectacular. Taken together, they've certainly made me wonder whether I have, from time to time, caught glimpses of the future, or have come to know things by some method other than the traditional five senses. A very small number of such incidents have led me to make decisions that ultimately affected my life in dramatic and positive ways.

It's only human to want to ascribe meaning to these kinds of events. I've had half a century to think about mine. The possible precognitions and flashes I've experienced fall into three broad categories of meaning:

1. Those that had no obvious practical value at all, where the possible precognitive aspects of the thought or dream became apparent only after the fact. That accounts for the vast majority of the cases.

2. Those that had some real value in guiding actual

decisions or advice in real time, ahead of the event being foreshadowed.

3. Those that served to bring me closer to another human being.

For the longest time, I considered the first category to be interesting but ultimately useless. Now, I'm not so sure. Two things those events did accomplish were to make me take the possibility of precognitive events seriously, and to be alert for them. This left me favorably disposed and sufficiently open minded to perceive, seriously consider, and then ultimately act on the one premonition that would matter most in my life, the one that led me to award myself a sabbatical in order to pursue my passion for writing, a step that was utterly necessary for me to feel fulfilled in life.

The value of categories 2 and 3 is obvious.

As I noted previously, if there is such a thing as a "talent" for extrasensory perception, or whatever you want to call it, I don't really think I have it. On a ten-point psi scale, I'd rate myself as no more than a 3 at very best. Certainly, I am no psychic. But if you think about it, the fact that I'm *not* adept at this kind of thing is more exciting than if I were. The implication is that *everyone* can do this at least a little—and probably does.

Have you never had a song go through your head, only to hear it pop up on the radio seconds later? Have you never reached for the phone intending to call someone, only to have it ring with that person calling you? Have you never had a word or a name appear in your head, and then come across that very word or name a short time later in real life? Have you never visited a new place, only to be overcome with a strong feeling that you'd been there before?

The whole purpose of language is to create symbols for experiences, things, and ideas, which can then be communicated. The most common experiences tend to get their own unique labels, and there's a well-worn two-

49

word French term for the last one I mentioned in the preceding paragraph. We name it precisely because it happens to nearly all of us. So when someone says the words "déjà vu," heads nod. No one looks perplexed because no one fails to understand the meaning. We've all felt it, or have known someone who has.

But why is that? How is it possible for a strange place or new experience to seem familiar? I don't presume to try to answer that. But the larger point is that whatever these events are or are not, the *feelings* they produce within us are real. And such feelings are more common than most people realize.

Case in point: Just fifteen minutes ago (relative to when I'm typing this) a friend of mine contacted me to tell me about a strange coincidence revolving around a certain word he'd just read in one of my novels. It's a word he had not thought about or spoken aloud in years, but it had just come up in a conversation in his home *the day before* he read it in my book. Weird, huh? But wait, there's more. Until just recently, I had not communicated with this friend in years. We came back into contact specifically because of my writing, which in turn happened only because I had acted on a premonition about my health. Are you beginning to see how this works? There are layers upon layers upon layers. We're lucky if we get to peel back *one* of them.

Earlier I mentioned the great Swiss psychotherapist and researcher Carl Jung. He observed so many instances of this type of phenomenon that he was moved to give it a name. Perhaps you've heard it; the term shows up from time to time in pop culture. Jung called it "synchronicity."

The basic idea is that there is some kind of force in, or feature of, the universe that leads to strange coincidences taking place. These coincidences may not be connected *causally* (only because it's hard to conceive how they might be) but Jung held that nevertheless they *are* meaningful. His theories along these lines generally are viewed as the first attempt by a serious scientist to embrace events previously held as the exclusive province of paranormal investigators.

The famous example he gave was a session where he and a patient were discussing her dream, which involved a scarab symbol. The scarab is an ancient Egyptian representation of a beetle, which that society revered as a symbol of the heavenly cycle of rebirth and regeneration. At the precise moment he and the patient were discussing the topic, Jung heard a tapping on the window. Care to guess what was trying to get into the room and join the therapy session? If you guessed a beetle, you're starting to get the picture.

Jung also believed that all humans, from infancy, can tap into a collective unconsciousness and retrieve universal concepts from it, in an *inherited* process similar to that of animal instinct. He didn't really try to explain how this process physically worked. But if he's right, then each of us somehow has access to data that do not come to us via any of the 5 senses that we know about. And this, as I said, was from a stone cold sober, very serious-minded scientist who had a profound impact on the field of psychoanalysis and who is still followed and widely respected today.

In trying to study these phenomena by way of my personal experiences, I don't really have much of a sample to work with. The full set of my anecdotes alone does not provide enough data to offer any kind of proof or draw any kind of meaningful conclusions. Fortunately, I'm not the only person in the world to have experienced these sorts of things. Far from it. The woods are filled with other people who've had far more dramatic and powerful psi experiences than mine. If the records and stories are to be believed—and this is not as big of an "if" as you might imagine, given the weight of the data—then the phenomena not only are real, but are common enough to be a basic part of the overall human experience, just as

Jung felt they were.

This leads to the obvious next question: What physical force or forces make such phenomena possible?

At the moment, no answer is forthcoming from the scientific community, because the consensus there is that these happenings are not objectively real and therefore are not to be taken seriously. That reaction is not difficult to understand. Science is a very rigorous and formal discipline. For a phenomenon to be successfully examined as part of the scientific process, it must lend itself to reliable observation and duplication in the laboratory. That's the way science works. Observations are made. Facts are gathered. An hypothesis is formed. The hypothesis is tested in the lab. If the test seems successful, other scientists try to duplicate it. Hypotheses that can't be tested with reliably duplicated results are judged to have little if any scientific merit.

Theories about paranormal events abound. But so far no one has been able to test any of them by way of successfully, reliably, and *predictably* reproducing psi events in the lab. However, when skeptical scientists make this point, they usually state it in such a way as to leave the impression that such phenomena *never* have been demonstrated in a lab setting. And that most definitely is not true. Despite the consensus among their peers that all things now classified as "paranormal" are pure fantasy, enough scientists have risked ridicule and career ostracization to study such phenomena that we now have an impressive amount of valuable data. Stanford University, Duke University, Princeton, UCLA and other respectable institutions have conducted serious research into parapsychology, with impressive results.

Even the steely-eyed CIA got into the act for a while. (Can you imagine? "Yes, I could mentally beam you that information. But then I'd have to kill you.") Experiments conducted by sober-minded researchers and carried out with scientific rigor have shown the existence, in lab conditions, of phenomena including various forms of clairvoyance, remote seeing, and psychokinesis. The card reading experiments carried out by Duke's J.B. Rhine and others were so conclusive that skeptics have rejected such tests pretty much on general principle, on the grounds that something must be wrong with them.

Paranormal experiments have been well summarized by other authors; there is no need for me to do that again here, although I certainly encourage you to look into this for further reading. (An excellent start for you would be *The Parapsychology Revolution*[8] by Robert M. Schoch, Ph.D., and Logan Yonavjak.) Some of the phenomena recorded have been stunning. But here's the rub. A given natural event, having appeared once, should appear again under identical circumstances. For example, if we conduct a lab test today and observe that water freezes at zero degrees Centigrade, then when we repeat the test tomorrow under the identical controlled conditions, water should freeze again at the same point. But with psi events, that is not what happens, to the endless frustration of researchers. Imagine what modern life would be like if no one had ever been able to duplicate Benjamin Franklin's experiment with the kite and key. Among other things, we wouldn't have harnessed electricity, and you'd be reading this book on your computer by candlelight (OK, that was a joke). Psi events do produce the occasional observable "lightning flash," so to speak. But because such events cannot be recreated at will even under identical conditions, mainstream science considers parapsychology to be a pseudoscience at best.

In some ways, it hardly seems fair. After all, "regular" science has its own mysterious and unexplained forces to contend with. Some kind of dark energy is causing the universe to expand. Equally mysterious dark matter gives form and structure to the galaxies. Scientists can write equations for both and can even tell you that the two combined make up more than 90% of the matter and energy of the universe. Yet they have no real idea what these things are. But because the effects of both can be reliably observed and measured, these phenomena fall into the realm of science, and appropriately so.

Nor are those the strangest unexplained phenomena that science has observed and accepted. Not by a long shot. In the last century, physicists discovered that some subatomic particles can pass right through solid barriers that should have been impenetrable, almost as if by magic. But when something so seemingly bizarre and ridiculous as the ability to pass through solid walls appears with predictable regularity in a science lab, it won't do to chalk it up to sorcery. Instead, scientists accept it and give it a name—which, in this case, was "quantum tunneling." And that is just one of the many crazy-house aspects of quantum physics. Some elementary particles exhibit all kinds of bizarre and enjoyable behaviors, up to and including being in two places simultaneously.

These things are not magic. They're simply processes and realities that were unknown, until such time as they became known. If you can formulate an hypothesis for it, write equations to describe it, and then reliably duplicate an event in the lab, it's as real is anything is ever going to get. The logic of these observations is unassailable: It happens, therefore it *can* happen.

The field of parapsychology also has documented objects passing through what was thought to have been impenetrable barriers, or even materializing out of thin air. Such occurrences are common with poltergeist events. If the sober, credible, reliable witnesses who have sworn to such events had been testifying about a murder instead, no one would have blinked at sending the accused to the gallows. But when it comes to attestations of eggs passing through a closed refrigerator door or a pebble materializing out of thin air, science laughs it off, no matter the number or caliber of the witnesses. The logic becomes, "It could not possibly have happened; therefore, it didn't." Or, to put it in more human terms, "That's crazy talk. And if you're going to persist in it, well, we know what that makes you."

The scientific rejection of credible observations seems unfair, but as noted there is a reason for it. Observations in, say, quantum physics labs are accepted, no matter how bizarre, because the same experiments produce the same results over and over. But that is not the case with paranormal events, where something that happens once may not happen again later even under identical conditions.

Still, predictability and repeatability issues notwithstanding, a reliable observation does produce facts, and those facts should not be denied just because they don't lend themselves to immediate explanation. Certainly thrusting one's fingers in one's ears won't make them go away. Yet science tends to do that. History is replete with incidents of respected scientists rejecting new ideas even in the face of strong evidence. And if you think this kind of negative knee-jerk reaction to new or uncomfortable facts ended with the persecution of astronomer Galileo Galilei in the 17th century, guess again. Very few scientific advances have failed to bring initial ridicule[9] to those responsible. Even the great physicist Stephen Hawking had to endure his share of derision earlier in his career. As recently as the 1960's, science was denying the existence of ball lightning despite numerous well-documented sightings throughout the world. Today ball lightning is generally acknowledged as real, even though it's still not satisfactorily explained and cannot be precisely reproduced in a lab.

With ball lightning, the logic seems clear enough: The phenomenon occurred, therefore it exists. But all too often that simple logic escapes the world of mainstream science. It's simply too easy, and too tempting, to write off that which does not fit into the officially endorsed and widely held notions of reality.

The acceptance of events currently classified as paranormal does not require belief in the supernatural, although at our present level of technology, the two concepts are very close in their semantic meaning. Science fiction writers have been observing for decades that to primitive cultures, high technology looks exactly like magic. Right now, paranormal events may seem that way to us. Really, they're no more magical than a laser beam, X-ray, or the amazing images that appear when you turn on the TV. Psi phenomena have been observed repeatedly, therefore they are real, and from there it follows that they must have natural causes rooted in forces and physical laws as solidly grounded as $E = mc^2$. We just haven't discovered those forces and derived those equations yet.

Someday, hopefully, we will. What we'll find is a matter for conjecture. But I strongly suspect we'll learn that our species—in fact, all life—is interconnected in ways that are not visible to the eye—or discernible to any of the accepted senses—just as Carl Jung suggested. (For some facts along those lines that may change your world view, read up on Edgar Cayce, the best documented psychic in history).

Can you imagine how human civilization might be different if we *were* to solve these mysteries, and make the scientific solutions a part of our everyday technology? What if, for instance, some enterprising open-minded scientist some day were to discover the laws of physics that come into play when a object appears to materialize out of thin air, as has been documented in some poltergeist events. He or she may have just discovered the secret to transdimensional interstellar travel. The very real evidence gathered to date not only shows that such materializations do happen, but also suggests that the process requires very little energy. What laws of nature drive that? In asking that question, we're Ben Franklin, as he observes a wonderful, mysterious, and somewhat frightening bolt of lightning, scratches his head, and says, "Gee? What's up with that?" Franklin had already taken the first three most important steps—seeing the lightning, accepting the lightning as real, and then realizing that there had to be a scientific explanation (and that it was not, for instance, a weapon of Zeus, as the ancient Greeks believed). With so called "paranormal" events, we only lack someone with the right kite, key, and properly open mind to discover what's going on.

But you don't have to understand the principles behind the lightning to accept that it exists. The same is true of ball lightning, which we don't understand but which we do know occurs. And that brings me back to my personal experiences with what might or might not be "paranormal" events. In no case can I explain what happened. Skeptics would say I cannot prove *anything* has happened to me at all, other perhaps than the fact that somehow I managed to develop a strong sense of intuition and personal insight. Certainly, I would like to think there's more to it than that. But what? If someone had been trying to send me a message through these events, who was at the other end of the line? God? A guardian angel? Could it, somehow, have been my future self, making sure I took the steps I needed to take to chase my life's dream while I still had time to do so? Or maybe it was, after all, nothing more than me talking to myself, making use of my own ability to peer into my own heart and soul to make sure I did what I needed to do.

For my purposes, such explanations do not matter. They're not necessary to make *use* of the phenomena. In 2013 there was an action that I needed to take. When the thought suggesting that course of action presented itself, I was receptive to it. I acted. My emotional life changed dramatically, and for the better. It did so because I got the message, and I listened.

Are you listening for yours?

# 6 THE SECRET LIFE OF DREAMS

In the dream, I'm working in a TV studio, participating in some kind of production. Someone asks me to create an on-screen graphic for the program. I agree to do so. The producer asks me whether I'm sure I'm capable of accomplishing the task. I answer, "It may not be as good as The Food Network, but I can do it."

A short time later the dream moves outdoors. The scene is one of civil unrest and warfare. Somewhere in the distance, a civil defense siren is going off. Men dressed in civilian clothes are standing next to me in the street, some of them carrying assault rifles. I understand, without knowing *how* I know, that they're involved in some kind of a rebellion or coup. Down the street is a barricade made of vehicles and car tires. As I watch, two jet fighters plummet from the sky and crash in the near distance, startling me. The man next to me turns and says, "It's time for a change."

At this point, I wake up. As I put on my robe and head downstairs for breakfast, I turn the dream over in my mind. The reference to the Food Network particularly puzzles me. Why would I say that, even in a dream? I am aware the Food Network exists but have never sampled more than about 15 seconds of it at a time, usually while flipping through to other channels.

In this frame of mind and with those thoughts on my mental projector, I open the morning paper. The first headline that catches my eye is, "Dozens dead in Odessa fire; gov't launches 1st offensive." The article, on page A1 below the fold, goes on to explain how Ukraine had finally launched military operations against separatists in the east. Insurgents fighting near the town of Slovyansk had succeeded in shooting down some government helicopters. *Two* of them.

Hmmn.

A few pages later, this headline catches my eye: "Food Network show races into Tucson." Page A11, above the fold. The Food Network, as it turns out, was in town shooting an episode of "The Great Food Truck Race." The production follows eight trucks as they race across the country, and the cast and crew just happened to be pulling into my city on this particular weekend.

The dream I just described happened last night, relative to when I'm typing the first draft of these words. Those articles appeared in the newspaper I read just this morning. Interesting, huh?

But wait. Here's an additional fun fact, thrown in at no extra charge. It was my intention to write this chapter earlier this week, but I've been struggling with how to start it. So, I decided to put it off a day, and I skipped on to chapter seven, leaving number six, this one, for today. Thanks to last night's dream, this morning I had no trouble figuring out how where to begin. How convenient! Even so, it's just coincidence, right? But if it *wasn't*, then the implications of me experiencing two new possibly precognitive dreams just when I needed them for my writing project are staggering.

I decided to devote an entire chapter to dreams because they're inextricably bound up with other concepts we've been discussing. Jung, who also wrote extensively about *his* dreams, knew this. Dreams and precognition seem to go hand in hand. It therefore stands to reason that if one has a vivid dream life, then one might also have an increased ability to experience the kinds of events to which this book is devoted. And throughout my life, my dream life has been quite extraordinary. In fact, I have grown to be more adept at certain exotic forms of dreaming with each passing year, as we'll see. A central point in this book is that if I can do these things, then anyone can. I hope to show you how you can benefit from what I've learned to enrich your dream life, too, if you care to do that.

One of the very earliest memories I have involves a probable dream; I wrote about it earlier, that incident where I thought I saw beings flying around outside my window, at an age so young I didn't yet have words to even begin to describe what I saw. The first major incident that ever struck me as possibly having *psychic* significance, and which led me to a lifelong interest in the subject, also involved a dream—the one I referenced in a previous chapter where, at the age of 15, I flew over a scene I had witnessed the previous night in a dream. This is the most interesting type of dream, one that somehow seems to visually preview something that hasn't yet happened. In my life I've only experienced a few "major" dream flashes or visions of this type. Much more common are dreams like the one summarized at the top of this chapter, those that do not *precisely* predict a given scene or event in fine photographic detail, but which nevertheless seem to have a correlation to a reality that I did not know about, or that had not yet taken place, at the time of the dream.

For me, it's this latter type that's much more common, and I experience them with great regularity. I call them "minor" flashes because they're not literal, and do not present the exact mental image of something I will later see. But even so, the close correlations to future reality can be damned spooky.

What is happening here?

The answer from skeptics, of course, is that nothing is going on. It's all just random chance and false correlations. Thoughts, ideas and images are flitting around our brains all the time. It's inevitable that some of them will, on occasion, seem to "match" something that later occurs. It's important to remember, the skeptics would argue, that correlation does not prove causation, or signify any real connection or significance at all.

I might even be inclined to accept that if it weren't for the handful of incidents I've experienced where a vision in a dream turned out to *precisely* match something that was about to occur. A close correlation is one thing. But getting a visual mental snapshot of a scene before I've physically laid eyes on it is quite another. Those few instances where this has happened to me have been so breathtaking that they've made me look more closely at the less spectacular, but much more common occurrences of "mild" foreshadowing that do not involve an actual vision, but only a concept, as in the Food Network example.

How might a precognitive event of this type physically occur?

The commonly accepted "rational" notion of the dream state is that it's largely a closed system, operating on data already in hand, with little or no new information coming in. This is due to the fact that the dreamer's sensory input mostly has been shut down. The components of the mind acting as the dream's director, set designer, and script writer all operate on data that, for the most part, the brain already ingested at some point in the past. The sleeper's unconscious mental processes are creating a dreamscape, and telling a story, drawing on building blocks of knowledge and information pre-existing within this closed system.

Usually the dream machinery will assemble the blocks into familiar structures and concepts. For example, when

Freud had dreams containing travel references, he saw carriages, not cars, because that's what he knew about. Put another way, if you're a surgeon, I'd venture to guess you have a lot of dreams about medicine. I'm a TV guy, and so many of my dreams are set in TV newsrooms. Dreams of this nature are like a novel—they're not "real" but are realistic.

Sometimes the dreamscape will be surreal, but even then it will be based on concepts already in hand. In other words, you might dream of a planet with purple soil and a sky filled with red stars. That doesn't mean any such environment actually exists. The dreamscape is not realistic. However, the concepts of purple, red, soil, stars, and sky were already on hand in the dreamer's mental database.

In a similar fashion, if you're a guy, you might conjure up a dream involving a romantic relationship with an old girlfriend. The woman is not really there, of course. She's just your mind's mental concept of her, constructed from the way you remember that person's appearance and behavior. Events take place based on your mind's understanding of how such things can work. If you're lucky (in the dream, that is) you might get to break some of life's rules, but those rules are still there, in the background. The dream is operating within a framework based on a lifetime of your real-world sensory input and observation.

Or perhaps you might dream of a woman you've *never* met. Now your mind has constructed a new image of a woman based on its understanding of what women are like. In this case, the character is entirely fictional, constructed from whole cloth. But even so, the dreamer's onboard database provided the raw material. The dream woman has no parallel in the real world because the dream-making machinery has no access to real-world data that have not already been received. It's a closed system.

*But what if it isn't?* What if new information somehow

*can* leak in—perhaps through the collective unconscious that Jung wrote about? How might that change things?

To get some insight into that question, examine what happens on those rare occasions when new information enters the dreamscape in real time. Even when someone is sound asleep, the senses are still providing data. During deep sleep the brain filters most of it out, and usually there's nothing significant to report anyway. So it simply doesn't register on the dreaming mind. But what happens when there *is* significant new data gives a clue as to how the dream machinery processes new information.

Example: You dream that you're slogging through deep snow, only to wake up and find that you've kicked off the covers on a chilly night. Your brain had received the sensory information that you're shivering cold. The unconscious part of you that's controlling your dreams took that information and morphed it into the dreamscape. Suddenly, you're cold in your dream. But the reason for the cold feeling as presented in your dream may differ dramatically from the real-world reason that led to the perception of cold. In other words, you don't dream you've kicked off the covers; instead, you dream that you're knee-deep in snow. Or, you're standing naked in a corporate boardroom. Or swimming in a cold stream. Or any number of scenarios involving cold and discomfort.

In a similar fashion, a real-life clap of thunder while you're sleeping might lead to a dream sequence involving a gunshot, or a crash, or an explosion, or the start of a race. Or the dog jumping onto the bed becomes a dream earthquake. I once had an entire dream sequence featuring a UFO invasion that turned out to have been triggered by sirens and a shotgun blast in my neighborhood as police tried to shoot out the tires on a stolen car they were chasing.

What's happening here is that your dreaming brain is taking in the data, but is using it symbolically, not literally, morphing it into something related or similar within your dreamscape.

Here's another example that I'm guessing may have happened to you, because it's happened to me and it shows up frequently in the dream literature: dream paralysis. When you enter certain deep stages of sleep, your brain disconnects most of your motor functions, which has the happy benefit of preventing you from acting out the scenes unfolding in your dreamscape. It would not do, for instance, to go running out of your bedroom to catch a football that's been tossed to you in your dream Super Bowl game. The disconnection leads to a partial state of paralysis.

Sometimes knowledge of this paralysis leaks into the dreamscape. What happens? The dreamer has a nightmare. Maybe you're trapped in a burning car and can't move. Maybe you're stuck in quicksand. Maybe someone is about to kill you and you're frozen with fright. Perhaps the dream is even more literal—you picture yourself in bed, as you actually are, unable to move in the face of some evil entity that is approaching, or perhaps has already arrived and is holding you down.

Those are the kinds of dreams that tend to cause one to wake up screaming. But like the milder non-nightmare forms of sense-prompted dreaming, they're based on the principle I'm talking about: Sensory perception leaks into the dreamscape and then gets morphed into an alternate dream reality that builds upon that initial real-world sensory cue and elaborates it into a story.

So that we can keep track of what we're talking about, let's call this process of incorporating real incoming data symbolically into the dream environment as Dreamscape Data Morphing, or DDM.

Now consider this: What if the dreamscape were able to receive, at least on occasion, *other* kinds of real-life information—information that somehow manages to arrive via some pathway *other* than the traditional five senses we know and accept?

Let's say, for instance, that someone you care about who's living in another city is having a crisis of some sort. Your dreaming brain somehow receives this information. Through our newly defined DDM process, your brain brings in the data and synthesizes it into the dreamscape, just as it would with data from the other five senses. Now, suddenly, you're dreaming about this individual. Perhaps the person in the dream scenario is even in some kind of trouble. In any case, you wake up the next morning with the thought of this person weighing on your mind. Accompanying that may even be a sense of concern or alarm. Conceivably you might even make a phone call or send off an email or Facebook message because of it—at which point you are astonished to learn that your friend has had a car wreck, or has suffered a heart attack, or is going through some other kind of physical or emotional trauma.

You didn't have a vision. The dream wasn't literal in the sense that you clairvoyantly saw the person actually lying in a hospital bed connected to a heart monitor, or whatever else the real-life situation might have been (although such literal visions do sometimes occur, too). And yet somehow you received information you had no normal way of getting, to which your dream responded, which in turn caused you to have waking thoughts of this person and perhaps take action.

As noted previously, this precise thing has happened to me more than once. I'm willing to bet that it's happened to you, too, and that when it did, you either tossed it off, or decided to keep it to yourself.

Now let's examine the two dreams I set forth at the top of this chapter in light of this theoretical process. What *could* have happened was that my dreaming brain somehow glommed onto the fact (perhaps through that collective unconscious that Jung wrote about) that violence had begun in Ukraine, and that two aircraft had crashed as a result of it. My brain then ingested that data and transformed it, through the Dreamscape Data Morphing process, into a dream scenario for me. The dreamscape was not literal; note that in the dream I saw two jet fighters crash, not two helicopters. I have no way to know whether the person I talked with in the dream was real, and I suspect he wasn't (especially given the fact that he spoke English without a trace of accent). But still, when I woke up I was thinking of violent civil unrest, and as it turns out, violent civil unrest had erupted while I was sleeping.

In a similar fashion, perhaps my sleeping brain somehow received information that the Food Network was in town—or maybe it only learned that I was about to read a newspaper article about the Food Network. It created a dream scenario for me utilizing the concept. It wasn't literal; I did not wake up knowing that the show was coming to town. But I did wake up thinking about the show, a program to which I had never devoted an iota of thought at any previous time, and had no obvious reason to be doing so now.

And then there also is the possibility that your dreaming brain might receive real-world extrasensory data and then present it to you quite literally. That has happened to me on a handful of occasions, which I presented earlier, including one in which I saw a former dear friend of mine suffering from a very specific physical affliction that had not yet even occurred.

I doubt that in any of these cases my brain or any other entity was deliberately trying to "send me a message," any more than the sight you behold when you open your eyes and view the sunrise is an attempt to send you one. The sleeping brain simply saw what it saw, and responded as it always does. I won't try to delve any further than Jung already did into an explanation of how such data are transmitted, but I submit that there is sufficient evidence to suggest that these events do happen. And, like Jung, I believe they have meaning.

Of course, you can always laugh it off and retreat to the more "reasonable" explanations that it's all just coincidence, fantasy, hallucination, etc. As noted, I cannot prove such views wrong. But a brusque dismissal of these phenomena on those grounds runs the danger of missing a very important point, and it's this: Regardless of the source or cause of these phenomena, the feelings they produce within the human mind and heart are very real. Therefore no understanding of the human experience can be complete without acknowledging events of this type.

If my DDM hypothesis is right, then dreams do have some practical utility. But for the rest of this chapter, we will discuss a completely different aspect of dreams, and it's this: they're fun. Not only are they fun, but we can learn how to make them *more* fun. I did. And I believe that by helping you to retrace my footsteps, you can learn these principles, too, if you have an interest in doing that and are willing to work at it.

Let's start with this: Do you fly in your dreams?

I do. But I didn't always.

Researchers have studied this kind of thing. One study found that slightly over half of people who are willing to answer questions about dreaming report having had at least one "flight" dream[10]. Some researchers classify "endlessly falling" as the same thing as flying, which it most definitely is *not*; the latter involves conscious direction, but the former doesn't. In any case, it appears the experience of willful flight within dreams is not precisely rare, but nor is it particularly frequent or something that most people experience a lot of.

Speaking personally, the number of people with whom I've been familiar enough to ask about dream flight is not large, but I can report that I've only met a very small handful of people who would admit to it.

I fly in my dreams not quite every night or even every week, but with great regularity. And here's the thing: I *learned* to do it. It is, in fact, a form of lucid dreaming, which we'll be talking about in more detail.

When I was a young boy—in the 4th grade or thereabouts—I had a dream in which I jumped into the air while playing in my front yard, and then seemed to hang there for an instant looking down, before slowly drifting back to the ground. The moment seemed kind of magical, and as you can see it stuck with me. (This is the same year I had to be rushed to the hospital for an emergency appendectomy, from which I still bear a scar. It's also the same year I had that vision of a skull hanging on the wall. I mention this only because many of my most memorable dream and/or possibly psi-related events have been associated with medical trauma involving anesthesia—a connection other researchers might want to explore further).

I began to wonder if it would be possible to teach myself to fly in dreams. I worked on it for a long time. My primary method was to dwell on it while lying in bed. During the time just before drifting off to sleep, I would imagine myself flying low over the ground and then soaring up into the air. The funny thing is, it worked. It didn't happen right way. But within a few years, I was regularly flying in dreams.

At first, I didn't get very high, just a couple of feet. The sensation was much like scooting along with your feet just above the bottom of a pool. But I got better and better at it. At this point in my life, I regularly make it up to the cloud tops. Interestingly, in very few of these dreams do I actually know that I'm dreaming at the time. Yet I become aware that for some reason, flight is possible at that moment, and so I attempt it.

I did not realize it at the time, but the art of manipulating what goes on in your dreams is very special. Through having read about and researched the experiences of others, I now know that any such impact of the conscious mind on the dreamscape is a form of what's called "lucid dreaming." So when, as a young boy, I taught myself to fly in my dreams, I was conducting my first experiments with that.

My next experiment came a few years later. After my success with dream flight, after a while I began to wonder if it would be possible to make myself fully conscious within a dream, and to wake myself up. Again, I was too young to grasp the significance of the concept of "lucid dreaming." I had done no reading on the subject at that time. But I always enjoyed dreaming, and it seemed logical that the more power I had over the process, the more enjoyment I could extract.

So I began experimenting with the idea. I did it the same way I'd learned to fly: Before drifting off to sleep I would rehearse scenarios in which I would (1) begin to suspect that I was dreaming, which I would then test by (2) imagining, within the dream, that I was lying in bed; at which point I would then (3) attempt to sit up in bed.

I have to report at this point that, unlike my experience in teaching myself to fly, this experiment led to some unpleasant consequences. Specifically, I did learn to become conscious that I was dreaming, but instead of always succeeding in waking myself, what I often did was to surface into consciousness or semi-consciousness trapped within a body that was frozen with the aforementioned state of dream paralysis.

As noted, such an experience can be quite unpleasant. When you "surface" from your deep dream into that paralyzed body, you're half in and half out of the dream world. Time seems to stand still, dragging out the trapped feeling for what seems like an eternity, thereby adding to the unpleasantness. It's quite easy to lapse into a state of panic. The sensation is not unlike what I'd imagine drowning or suffocating to be, and when I've experienced it, it seems to take me forever to fight my way out of it.

Eventually, I did succeed in waking myself up in this fashion. But I can't say it was fun. So after proving to myself that I could do it, I ceased with that line of experimentation. And that is probably why many years passed before I tried to take the next logical step—which is, of course, to try to walk around in a dream and manipulate your surroundings *without* waking up.

There is no obvious reason why anyone should not be able to do that. The entire dreamscape, after all, is a world of *your* making. It's a stage on which you are the director, playwright, set designer, and lead actor. Your unconscious mind is calling all the shots—not just for what you do, but for what others there in the dream with you are doing as well. It even controls the dream weather! Why *shouldn't* your conscious ego be able to take control of all that? Think of what fun it would be if you could!

About five years ago I started experimenting with this—the idea being to become aware that I was dreaming, but this time not to wake myself up. The results were, for me, spectacular. The process for bringing this off consist of three basic steps: (1) Learning to recognize that you are dreaming; (2) passively participating in the dream process as a spectator while consciously reflecting on what you are seeing, followed by; (3) taking active steps, initially small, to manipulate the dream environment without waking yourself up.

Step one: How do you know when you're dreaming?

That is a hard one to answer. But it has to do with recognizing that the things you're seeing can't possibly be real. Most dreamscapes have fundamental flaws that separate them from everyday reality; the key here is to develop a willingness to challenge what you see. The way to develop *that* habit is to do it in your waking world, too. What I did was to get into the practice of asking myself, every few minutes, this question: Is what I'm seeing real? And how do I know? At the same time I would ask myself that question, I would clasp my right hand onto something or knock on something, whatever was near. Thus I developed a repetitive routine: Question, grab. Question, grab. If you do such a thing regularly, then what I found (and research has shown me that others have stumbled onto the same technique) is that the habit carries over into your dream reality. (As an interesting side note, once I got into the habit of dream flying, I learned to recognize that the act of doing so proved I was dreaming.)

Step Two: Now, let's say you've done the "dream testing" outlined as part of step one, and have come to the realization that you are dreaming. What's next? In my earlier experiments where I tried to wake myself up, I envisioned my consciousness retreating to my sleeping body and then trying to surface to an awake state from there. To remain dreaming after having realized that's what you're doing, visualizing yourself as sleeping is the *last* thing you want to do. In fact, what I learned is that you need to take care not to jolt yourself more awake! I found that treading softly, as it were, and avoiding strong emotional and physical reactions while simply observing my surroundings helped to keep me rooted in the dreamscape.

So—there you are. You're dreaming. You know you are. Now think of the possibilities. This is your world. You created it. You can make it do anything you want it to do! Now is the time to move beyond simple conscious dreamscape awareness. Which leads to: Step Three. Give dreamscape manipulation a try.

But here's a hint. One of the things that makes dreams so enjoyable is that they feel, at the time they're unfolding, like they're very real. The more you manipulate the dreamscape, the less real it might feel to you. In other words, if you have a normal non-lucid pleasurable dream, you might wake up feeling almost as if you had actually experienced something. But the more you manipulate the dream through the lucid dreaming process to create the pleasure, the less real it's going to feel. It can be like the difference between holding your own hand, and having someone else hold it. I found the key is to provide little nudges, rather than to try to exert godlike powers.

Before arriving at that philosophy, though, I certainly did find that godlike powers were possible, although now I rarely try to manipulate the dreamscape so dramatically. Here's an example, though, of what such powers can look like when utilized to their fullest extent.

Dreams tend to come in two varieties, or at least mine do—those that follow the laws of physics, thereby presenting a dreamscape that has the look and feel of everyday life, and those that don't. This example falls into the latter category. I dreamed I was in my car, falling from a height of about a mile over a desert landscape. I knew I'd die when I hit the ground, but I wasn't afraid. But then I said, "Wait a minute. This can't be real. I must be dreaming. I'm going to take charge." And I did. The first thing I did was to arrest the fall of the car. Then I leveled it off. And then I began rotating the car clockwise on its long axis. I did this because I was curious to see what would happen to the dream picture—the image of the earth and sky visible through the windshield in front of me. Every detail of the view was absolutely perfect as it rotated, and I remember marveling at that. Not a pixel was out of place. The horizon tilted, became vertical, and then the sky was where the earth and been. The mountains that had been below now projected down from above, with perfect, flawless, Technicolor clarity. The horizon continued to turn as I sat amazed at my own special effects prowess. Then I decided to wake up. When I opened my eyes, I was lying on a lounge chair in a garden. The air was crisp; yellow, orange and red leaves were falling all around me, making little whispering sounds as a gusty breeze whisked them along the ground. The house and garden were in no way familiar to me, but inside the home, I knew, was my mother (who as of the time of the dream was no longer living). Still very aware that I was dreaming, I walked inside, said hello, drank some coffee, made some small talk, and then told her I had to go. I then made another conscious effort to wake myself up, and this time I succeeded, opening my eyes to find myself lying awake in my own bed. When all was said and done, I'd had a dream within a dream in which I had been fully lucid, was able to completely and magically manipulate my surroundings at the lowest level before consciously moving to a higher level, and then leave the dream state altogether when I was ready to do so. That was extraordinary.

Here's another. The setting was a nuclear war. This sounds scary—but in part because of the skills I've developed, in this particular scenario I knew right away that I had to be dreaming. Now a vessel somewhere at sea in the direction behind me fired a missile toward a city over the horizon in front of me. The passage of the rocket overhead was incredibly loud, and the crackling roar split the sky with 3-D realism as the missile traveled from behind me toward the target in front of me, culminating in a blinding flash of light. I thought: "Wow. Stereoscopic sound! So loud and so real that my skin had rippled! This dreamscape has some amazing sound equipment! I want to experience that again!" So I did. I "ran the video again," as it were, marveling at just how realistic the experience was, even though I was fully aware that I was only dreaming. And once again, I was amazed at how, even though it was only a creation of my own mind, I was fully immersed in the experience with all dream senses engaged even more vividly than they would be in real life. The experience was completely realistic—but I knew it wasn't *real*.

I now know, of course, having done research on the topic, that lucid dreaming is not an uncommon experience. This leads me to believe that anyone who cares do so can learn how to experience it and to get better and better at it. I do it mainly for fun. Whatever else dreams might be, they're certainly a form of entertainment potentially more powerful than any movie. And you're the producer. So it makes sense to fully explore the medium, and perhaps see if you can exert some measure of control over what happens. But not too much! The surprise and wonder that some dreams provide when they're on autopilot is most of the fun.

But there are practical uses for this technique, too. For one, some believe that dreams are a window to the soul— or at least to the dreamer's mental state. Thus, through dreams a trained expert can evaluate mental health issues. There's a whole science dedicated to dream interpretation. I don't know whether I buy the idea that certain dream symbols and scenarios have specific meanings. But I do accept that dreams can give strong hints into the dreamer's personality, emotional issues, and mental challenges. Much has been written on dream interpretation, but it's not my purpose to delve into any of that here. Suffice it to say that there are several accepted schools of thought and that some of them conflict with one another. I prefer to merely enjoy the experience and not to try to extract some hidden meaning from it. (If you are curious to know more, I suggest the following: *The Dimensions of Dreams*[11], by Ole Vedfelt, published by Fromm International New York, 1999.)

That said, there is one other potential use for lucid dreaming, in my view, and it's this: If, for the sake of argument, the dreaming mind is more able to take in information that leaks in from the real world by some pathway other than the five known senses, then think about the power of coming across that stream of information while *conscious* within the dream. My work exploring that possibility has only just recently begun, and given my current medical situation, it's likely I won't get very far with it. Consider this your invitation to try it yourself.

So—how can you learn to have your own lucid dreams?

I've told you about how I got there. And I mentioned that it took me some time to master the steps. But I've also learned that it might be possible to take a shortcut to lucid dreaming in one particular scenario, and it's this one: the afternoon catnap.

Now, if the truth is to be told, I have always been enamored of naps. When I was a little boy, way before kindergarten, my mother would put me down for a quick afternoon nap, and I would not want to get up. I loved my naps. But Mom grew so alarmed at the difficulty in rousing me that she finally banned daytime naps altogether.

I started to indulge myself again a few years ago on those Saturdays and Sundays where the opportunity would present itself. And I learned something interesting. If I'm feeling drowsy, which I usually am in mid afternoon (as I observed earlier, it sucks to get old), then once I put my head down for the nap, I fall asleep very quickly. By contrast, at my actual bedtime I tend to toss and turn a lot, and I sleep very lightly for most of the night. But when I lie on my back while taking a catnap, I usually go under very quickly.

I learned that if I consciously monitor this process, many times I can take my consciousness into the dream state *with* me. In fact, I can move up and down between the two worlds, passing from one to the other kind of like a submarine—diving deep, partially surfacing, or surfacing completely. A "deep" dive is one in which I'm fully asleep and am not aware of my sleeping body, but am nonetheless conscious. A partial submergence is one in which the stream of dream images continues to project itself onto my mental screen (which is not a perfect analogy because I am immersed in the experience, same as any other dream) but I am at least dimly aware that I am lying on my back with my head on the pillow. And by "dimly aware" I mean that although the fact that I'm lying in bed does register on my consciousness, the dreamscape often unfolds on a different time scale, and an entire real-world hour can pass in the span of what seems like two dream minutes. In either partial or deep lucid dream submergence of this type, I am able to manipulate the dreamscape. And, interestingly, the problem of sleep paralysis does *not* present itself during such a nap. I'm able to fully surface at will, without going through that.

Perhaps your experience of sleeping is different from mine. But I have heard others report similar nap experiences. I am of the belief that even in normal nighttime sleep, the dreamscape's time scale is not perfectly synchronized with the real world. But during naps, the time slippage seems more pronounced, allowing the dreamer to move more quickly between worlds, thereby presenting a quicker route to lucid dreaming for those with the proper skills.

Give lucid dreaming a shot and see what happens. The results just might amaze you. And who knows what insights you might bring back?

So, if you're inclined to try this, here's a checklist.

### Steps for Lucid Dreaming

1.  Get into the habit of continually testing "reality" by challenging what you see and touch in the waking world. Develop a regular rhythm of questioning and touching, questioning and touching, a practice that should hopefully carry over into your dream world. Be patient. It could take a while; perhaps, a long while. (Learning to skillfully manipulate your dreams can, in fact, be a lifelong process). You'll know you've reached your first critical milestone when you arrive at a point when suddenly you're standing there, and you *know* it's a dream.

2.  When that happens, keep calm. Avoid strong emotions or strenuous physical activity, which could have the effect of waking you up (which you definitely do not want to happen if your sleeping body is in a normal state of sleep-induced motor paralysis). Breathe slowly. Savor the moment.

3. In trying to manipulate your lucid dreamscape, start small. Take a baby step. A good one is to jump a foot into the air, and see if you can delay your return to earth. On successive nights or lucid occasions, try to develop this into an ability to dream fly.

4. Once you have become able to dream fly, try other techniques for manipulating your dream environment. Really, there is no limit to your lucid dream powers. But like developing any other skill, it takes patience and practice. And remember, the more power you exert over your dream environment—especially when it comes to interactions with those you meet there— the less "real" the dream experience might seem to you upon awaking. (As with waking reality, surprise in finding out what people are going to do is half the fun!)

5. Experiment with afternoon catnaps. Try remaining aware of your reclining body as the dream state overtakes you. See if you can move yourself between the various levels of sleep while remaining lucid.

6. In any lucid dream state, look for data (words, images and thoughts) that might have some correlation to the real world. Have an open mind about such possibilities. When you wake up, inquire about anything unusual that strikes you. You will likely find that most such dream impressions have no obvious real-world correlation. But every now and then, if you are lucky, you might stumble on a gem of information that really does have a connection to an actual event that you didn't previously know about (as when I dreamed of my former friend who was ill, and was about to become even more ill).

7. When you do wake up, do not jump out of bed right away and go about your business. Upon first surfacing from a deep sleep, you may still have one foot, as it were, in the dream world. Linger for a moment. Take some time to review your dreams in your mind before

you do anything else. This sets the memories into place; otherwise, you could lose them. Keep writing materials at your bedside. If you have a remarkable dream, write it down while the memory is still fresh. You'll thank yourself later.

The last point I'm going to make before closing this chapter is this: I've read that some people who have experimented with lucid dreaming and researched the topic suspect that dream flying may be a form of out-of-body experience. I am agnostic on this point. But that said, even in my dreams, when flying I stay close to home.

Good luck!

# 7 MY THREE MIRACLES

Yes. I have experienced miracles. If not for two of them, you would not be reading this book, because in one scenario, I would have been dead since 1976, and in the other, even had I survived that critical year, I never would have found time to write it.

If you are a person of faith, I'm guessing you're at least willing to believe that what I'm saying might be true. If you're not, you may be tempted to brand me as a whackjob and toss the book aside, angry that you've wasted your time with it to this point. If that's the reaction you find welling up within you, please bear with me for just a moment longer. My goal in this book is to set forth principles that can work for any average person, without regard to whether that person is religious. Also remember that my background is as a sober-minded and award-winning mainstream media journalist, not as a carnival barker, while I take a paragraph to explain what I mean by "miracle."

The word actually has two definitions. One requires belief in God. The other only requires acceptance of facts.

Definition One, quoting from The Free Dictionary as presented online: "An event that appears inexplicable by the laws of nature and so is held to be supernatural in origin or an act of God." Definition Two, quoting from the same source: "One [an event] that excites admiring awe; a wonderful or amazing event, act, person, or thing."[12]

A commonly understood component of the concept of "miracle" in both cases is that it's something that works to benefit one or more people. In other words, it brings about something good. So, for the purpose of this discussion, my definition of the word "miracle" is this: something astounding and improbable that benefits one or more human beings, and happens right when it is most needed. If you are a person of faith and you believe miracles come exclusively from God, then hang on to that; I certainly would not try to dissuade you from your belief. If you're agnostic, atheistic, a secular humanist, and so on, you don't have to believe that anything supernatural is going on to appreciate, or even stand in awe of, certain highly improbable beneficial events and the effects they have on people, both physically and emotionally.

Having come with me this far, you already know about one of my three miracles: In 2013 I listened to my inner voice and changed my life in order to accomplish what I wanted to do while I still had time remaining in which to do it, not knowing when I made the decision that time indeed was running out. This actually is the *least* of the three events I want to tell you about here.

What I'm about to present to you are straight facts. I'm the only witness to these events, and you certainly are entitled to keep that in mind as you form your opinions. I believe my journalistic credentials, as previously submitted, suggest a high degree of credibility, but I leave that judgment to you. Only one of the events was even theoretically objective, in the sense that had anyone been with me, they would have seen what I saw. The other two exclusively involve personal feelings and intuition, thereby making them entirely subjective and completely unverifiable by anyone who was not standing in my shoes.

This, too, is a factor you are completely entitled to consider. The only thing I can do is raise my hand and swear by all that's holy and good that what I am about to relate is the full truth as I experienced it.

And lastly before we begin, as I've already hinted I will not ask you to believe that anything I'm about to tell you was done by the hand of God. It is not fashionable these days to try to foist religious beliefs on anyone, and I will not do that. Instead, I invite you to make up your own mind. But I will say this: If there is a God and if He does sometimes decide to intercede in human affairs, I have never seen anything to convince me that He acts today in any way that directly violates the laws of nature that He created. In that context, a "miraculous" event, even if it were the result of some kind of divine intervention, would present itself as nothing more than something incredibly improbable that nevertheless did manage to happen just when it was most needed. In other words, we're talking about odds and probabilities here, but not about observable "magic" or anything like it. Rolling the dice and having the cubes pause in mid-air, float down to the table, and then come up all sixes would be wondrous indeed. But having them come up all sixes again and again *without* appearing to have been directly manipulated would be only slightly less amazing.

The events I'm going to lay out for you now are incredibly personal. I have not shared them with more than four or five other people over the course of my entire life. This story will be hard for my friends and family to hear, for which I ask their understanding and forgiveness (I did tell my wife that I planned to do this, and she gave me her full and heartfelt support). But given that I only have a short time remaining ahead of me and no reputation to ruin with potential employers, now seems a good time to finally come out with this. I'm not doing it because I'm feeling an irrational impulse to expose myself emotionally to the world. For whatever reason and by whatever means (even if it was, as skeptics will insist, just a function of random chance) I wound up receiving an incredible gift. I believe others can benefit from the story of how that came about, and from learning what I did with that gift after receiving it. It would be a terrible, unforgivable waste to take this secret with me to my grave. The incredible facts must be shared.

Strap yourself in. This is a tough one. If you know me, you're going to hear about a side of me that you never suspected existed, and my guess is it will shock you. Even if you don't know me, this may be hard for you to hear.

Ready?

The year is 1976. I had just turned 19 years old. I'd always been what you might call a "good" kid—decent grades in school, no alcohol, no drugs, no trouble of any kind. But I was morose, self-centered, introverted, and prone to bouts of depression, which could at times be severe. Three months or so before the incident I'm about to relate, my lifelong asthma flared up into a crisis that put me in the hospital and nearly killed me (my lips and fingernails turned blue-black). After surviving that, my doctor put me on a pill comprised of the standard asthma medications ephedrine and theophylline, along with— unbeknownst to me at the time—Butabarbitol. The latter was type of barbiturate, which wound up in an asthma drug under the theory that stress leads to asthma attacks and can also prolong them. For similar reasons, my doctor prescribed a separate course of the popular sedative Valium. After my breathing crisis, I wound up on a regimen of taking *both* pills every four hours. I couldn't stop or even slow down; every time the drugs started to wear off, heavy wheezing of the type that had led to my ER trip began to return.

So there I was, a depressed teen experiencing raging hormones, now taking, around the clock, both Valium *and* an asthma drug laced with a mood-altering habit-forming barbiturate that would later come to be associated with adverse psychiatric side effects. I did it because that's what a doctor I and my family had trusted for years told me to do in order to be able to breathe.

During this same time, I was involved in a tumultuous teen romance. On one particular night, it went spectacularly bad, and the news came crashing down on me all at once. I'd gone from being head over heels in love (or so I thought) to feeling totally abandoned. The emotional pain was nothing like anything I had ever felt before. The word "despair" doesn't begin to cover it. The mental agony and grief were more than I could physically stand, and very suddenly I totally understood why some people throw themselves off buildings or into the paths of oncoming buses or trains.

So I tried to kill myself. And here's where the telling gets rough. But I have to share the details so that you can fully understand just how extraordinary the years since that time have been.

First, after asking Jesus to forgive me, I downed both bottles of my medicine *plus* an entire bottle of Lithium that my mother had given me. 36 hours later, I woke up, bitterly disappointed to be doing so.

Next, I went to the medicine cabinet and gobbled down every bottle of pills I could find, and drank every potion that looked remotely dangerous. One bottle, which was three-quarters full of some kind of green liquid, actually had a little skull and crossbones printed on its label. Within two hours, I had barfed it all up. I then passed out and was unconscious for another 24 hours or so.

When I woke up the second time, I decided that half measures would not do. I pulled down my father's pistol from his closet shelf and took it to my room.

Let me say again that the emotional pain I was feeling was absolutely unbearable, or so it seemed to me. It wasn't that I wanted to die. It was just that I absolutely had to end that pain. If you haven't felt such mental anguish, then you should thank God for that—but there really is no way to explain it to you. In the hospital, nurses sometimes will ask you to rate the physical pain you're feeling on a scale of 1 to 10. I have passed kidney stones twice; they say even people burned over 90% of their bodies who've also experienced kidney stones rate the latter as far worse. So if being burned alive is a 9, and kidney stones are a 10, then the mental anguish I was experiencing was about a 1,000. I tried to end my life for the same reason that someone jumps out of a high window to escape a burning room; it's not that you want to be dead, but it's the only thing you can think of to do to in the face of unbearable agony.

So, once again, I prayed for Jesus to forgive me. Then I pointed the gun at my chest and pulled the trigger.

Nothing happened.

I tried again. Still nothing.

And *again*. It misfired for a third time.

Putting the gun aside, I went to my father's bathroom, retrieved a razor blade, grabbed a large basin, took both to my room, and then slashed both wrists. After 30 minutes, I had filled the basin but the bleeding had stopped. And I wasn't so much as feeling light headed.

I had no choice at that point but to go find my mother and ask her to take me to the emergency room. And an hour later, there I was, a suicidal, idiotic kid sitting on a gurney getting his wrists stitched up, while on the other side of the curtain next to me a woman undergoing a severe asthma attack was fighting hard to live. The irony did not escape me. But my despair was so deep that I really didn't dwell on it. When I got home, I couldn't think of anything other to do other than to go to bed, and so I did.

Slowly, slowly over the course of the next few days, the despair began to lift ever so slightly. And that's when I began to wonder what the hell had just happened. A pistol misfired *three times*? Really? I pulled the shells out of the cylinder and examined them. Each had little marks on the percussion cap where the firing pin had struck with just enough force to leave a visible indentation, but not with enough force to set off the fulminate of mercury inside.

That sure got me thinking. I began to wonder whether my prayer just before pulling the trigger had made some kind of difference. And then as that train of thought rolled on, I had to ask myself why I was still living. Was I here for some kind of purpose? I've since learned that such thoughts are by no means uncommon for people who have survived against improbable odds. I didn't reach any conclusions, but what I did do was this: I swore a mighty oath to myself and my God that I would never, ever, *ever* do anything like that again.

Now at this point, you have to be thinking: That gun was defective, right? Or the bullets were faulty. The gun didn't fire because it *couldn't* fire. End of story. Right?

About two years later, I took the pistol out to my uncle's house, and we fired off a few rounds (of course, he had no idea why I wanted to test it; in fact, to this day only about three other people on earth know this story. Even my parents didn't know). Yes, honesty compels me to admit that the gun did misfire about twice in a dozen shots. But not on the first attempt. Not on the second. And not at any point consecutively.

Even so, we've established that the gun had a mechanical issue. So now, the skeptics would argue, we're dealing with probabilities, not miracles. Not to put too fine a point on it, they'd say, but I simply got lucky.

*But what luck!* A gun that I needed to misfire not just once, not just twice, but *three times in a row*, did, having never done so before that time or after. A family that needed to come into possession of a somewhat faulty gun rather than a reliable one, did (but not *too* unreliable; the last time it was called into action, prior to my incident, my mother used that same gun to reliably dispatch a deadly cottonmouth on the back steps of our house). A bottle of poisonous medicine sitting on a shelf that needed to have lost its potency had. A stomach that needed to be upset was. And possibly fatal asthma that had found every opportunity to strike before that point, despite being presented with the biggest stressor of my life, and in the absence of rescue medicine immediately afterwards (because I'd taken it all) decided to remain completely at bay. And all of these events, which needed to come together and present themselves at precisely the right moment in order to save my life, did.

But in a larger sense, if there was a miracle, those events were not it. The miracle was the life that followed—a life I nearly threw away. More on that in a moment.

So now you know the story of the worst night of my life. Now let me tell you about the *second* worst night. This tale is not quite so heavy, and there is even some humor in it, so you can relax at least a little bit. It was tough on me at the time, though, enough to test my vow never to resort to self-harm again. If I were going to break that promise, the night I'm about to relate definitely would have been it.

By the summer of 1979, I was still struggling with the depression, but I was off the Valium and the Butabarbitol. Instead, I was seeing an allergist who had prescribed different medications that didn't leave me drugged out of my mind.

I was still quite prone to depression, but I did have two things that brought joy to my life. One was my girl. The other was my car. I was crazy about both. In comparing my affections toward an inanimate object to my feelings for a human being, I would have been embarrassed just now to have inserted the adverb "equally" in the preceding sentence, so I didn't. Let's just say that if I'd been forced to choose between the two of them, I suspect I would have been struck with paralysis. But as I was about to learn, there are worse fates than having to make a tough choice.

For privacy's sake, I'm not going to say much about the girl except to note that my world revolved around her. Depression tends to make some people into kind of a butthead—not totally their fault, really, it's just hard to concentrate on the needs of others when you're completely absorbed in your own. I was already well advanced in buttheadedness even before I started struggling with my other issues (I'll accept the judgment of others about whether that has ever changed). But my point is that I still wasn't particularly stable emotionally, and my bad moments were awful. I was not exactly a daughter's mother's nightmare, but *I* wouldn't have wanted to date me.

At the same time, I had this car that I just adored. I can't rationally explain it. There is such a thing as a classic car, and then there's such a thing as an old car that runs good. This was the latter. My father brought it home for me as a replacement vehicle after some moron who thought "yield" meant "step on it" had creamed my Toyota. Dad was a car salesman, and the chief virtue of the vehicle he bought is that its value resided mainly in the weight of its salvageable metal, a fact that had allowed him to take it off the hands of his employer for a song. The old codger who'd traded it in had hung onto it like grim death long after all his friends had replaced the cars they'd bought during that same model year at least three times, maybe four.

The car I'm talking about was a 1961 tan Buick LeSabre 4-door sedan.

Okay, okay. I know. I loved it anyway. The words "Power Steering" quaintly arced across the metal steering wheel hub as if the concept had just been invented. It had factory air, which still blew cold. And best of all for a guy who was in love: bench seats with no pesky console in the middle. Now I could ride around town with my gal pulled close and my arm wrapped proudly around her. (You don't see *that* anymore. Kids today have no idea what they're missing). The car had a clock on the dashboard roughly in the shape of an eyeball, which hadn't run since 1962. I fixed it. Its AM-only radio ran on actual vacuum tubes. Two little civil defense triangles marked places on the dial where you could tune in for information in the event of nuclear war. How quaint was that? When this car rolled off the assembly line, the Cuban Missile crisis was a year into the *future*.

The car was equipped with an automatic transmission technology called Dynaflow. You absolutely could not detect the point which it transitioned from one gear into another. The engine was humongous by today's standards—an 8-cylinder 464 cubic inch monster. True, it only got about 8 miles to the gallon in the city. Who cared? Gasoline was only about 58 cents a gallon. The engine was so smooth that if you were sitting at a red light, you couldn't tell whether it was running.

The car would also turn out to have other advantages. On the rare occasions when Memphis got snow, the thing was so heavy that I would routinely just drive around smaller cars that were spinning their wheels or sliding off into ditches.

True, my particular car did have its flaws. Among them was that the hood had a splotch across it like someone had splashed battery acid on it. But the dealership crew had polished the vehicle to the point where you didn't notice the discoloration unless you were standing right over it. Sitting behind the wheel, what you saw were the sun, skies, and trees reflecting off the hood as you drove along in a stately fashion. And stately it was. The vehicle was so long and so heavy that it simply did not respond to bumps in the road. In motion, it was like floating along on a cloud.

My feelings toward the Buick were not rational. Young men and their cars. What can I say?

One night in the summer of 1979, my buttheaded ways finally caught up with me. The girl and I had a dispute which I ended by blowing up the bridge in a way that I'm embarrassed to have to recall. I will not retell it here except to say that nothing illegal, immoral, unethical or violent took place. But to have merely qualified as a jackass, I would have to have been five times nicer. When the echo of the last angry word had died in the air, the relationship had died with it, and I was fully aware that it would remain so for all eternity.

After the fight, I climbed into the beloved Buick to drive home alone. I was perfectly sober, I hasten to say. But my driving was fueled by anger, hurt, and grief. When I whipped down the exit ramp from I-240 and headed down Highway 61, I was going too fast by about 15 miles an hour. I scooted under the first couple of traffic lights, but then one turned yellow just as I was approaching it. I had to make one of those decisions about whether to go for it or stand on the brakes. I chose the latter.

The pedal sank to the floor. There was nothing.

At this point, I was beginning to regret the fact that I had not gotten around to taking the car in to have the emergency brake adjusted, because I knew that it was gone, too. I stomped on it anyway. The impact of my foot may have increased the forward momentum of the car, but other than that, there was no effect.

Now I was fast approaching the light. Cars had begun to enter the intersection. My life passed before my eyes. What to do?

The first thing I did was to step the transmission down, quickly going from drive to second to first. The engine drag bled away about half my speed, but I was still about to cross into the intersection.

To the right was a grocery store, which sat in a parking lot that had been carved out of a low hill. I swung the wheel again. The car veered into the lot, not quite on two wheels but nearly so. Now I found myself rocketing toward the retaining wall at the back of the lot. Another swing of the wheel, and now the car was zooming down an alley along the rear of the store. To my left was that high brick retaining wall. To my right was the brick wall that formed the back of the store. Looming in front of me was a giant commercial air conditioning unit. It was of the water-chilled variety and looked to me as if it had to weigh five tons.

What happened next is the type of thing that does make you wonder whether there is some kind of divine providence that looks after small children, imbeciles, and young hotheads who've just broken up with their girlfriends. Standing in front of that giant metal air conditioning unit were plastic milk jug crates—dozens and dozens of them, stacked at least six across, six high and four deep. Instead of smacking directly into that huge metal monster, which wasn't going to move, I was about to hit a collection of plastic boxes that consisted mostly of air. I couldn't have done much better if there'd been an equal volume of feather pillows piled there.

Before I even had time to think about it, the car hit. *Sa-MACK!* My head snapped forward, but I was prepared and had braced myself against the wheel.

After that loud report, there followed what seemed like several minutes of absolutely dead silence. Almost desultorily, I looked up. High in the air above my car were dozens of plastic milk crates. They'd just paused at the top of their ascent, and were now sitting there, like so many Wile E. Coyotes having just run off the cliff, pausing in mid-air and gazing at the canyon floor with woebegone expressions while considering what was about to happen. With the speed of molten caramel moving down the sides of a candy apple, the crates began to move in my direction. I can see the image now with crystal clarity, as if it were yesterday. *My poor car,* I remember thinking.

Then—BAM! BAM! BAM BAM BAM BAM BAMMITY BAM BAM BAM BAM BAM BAM BAM BAM BAM BAM BAM BAM BAM BAMMITY BAM BAM BAM BAM BAMMITY!

It was over. And when the last crate had bounced off onto the pavement and rolled away, the hood of my beautiful car had been transformed into a moonscape, and the windshield looked like the aftermath of a mob hit that had not gone well for the occupant. But I was completely uninjured.

An inspection later showed that the collision impact had moved that multi-ton chiller two feet across asphalt. But here providence smiled again. The unit had just been disconnected, and was not in use. It was just junk. The store manager was very forgiving. He didn't even charge me for the milk crates I had destroyed.

And that is how I came to lose the two things in life that I held most dear—my girl and my car—on the same night. Within the same 30 minute period, in fact.

Four hours later found me sitting in the dark atop the air conditioning unit at my house—more precisely, my parents' house, the home I'd grown up in and where I still lived—letting the comforting, roaring warm air blow up all around me as I sucked down an 8-pack of Miller ponies, one after the other. I don't recommend alcohol to get anyone through a crisis, but I didn't guzzle it and I didn't drink enough to get more than a mild beer buzz. I sat there for a long time and contemplated fate.

In the narrative above, I waxed more eloquently about the car, but trust me, all kidding aside, my feelings for the girl were far, far stronger. I felt as if I had been torn in two and had no hope of ever healing. I could feel the despair I'd experienced in 1976 welling up again within me. And yes, I did think about suicide that night. Boy, did I. I turned it over in my mind for several hours.

But ultimately, I rejected it. I did so because I'd made a promise. Mind you, I still hadn't figured out how and why I'd been able to walk away from my *last* bad night, two and a half years earlier. Why had I, of all people, been spared? At first glance, there didn't appear to be anything special about me. But at second and third glance, there *still* didn't.

I was a nobody, and not a particularly meritorious or deserving one at that.

Which brings us back to the question: What does it all mean? Why do things happen as they do?

Let's hold that thought for a moment longer, while I tell you about my *first* miracle.

This one falls into the category of "entirely subjective." If you've ever experienced anything like it, then you'll know instantly what I'm talking about. If you haven't, then the best my words will be able to do is to paint a very dim shadow for you of what happened.

The year was 1975, one year before my suicide attempts. The setting: Christian Brothers College (now Christian Brothers University) in Memphis.

I'm Catholic (a very lapsed one at the moment, sad to say, but I still define myself that way and I have always planned to go back to it once time allows). My parents provided me with a fabulous educational opportunity via enrollment at Christian Brothers High School in Memphis, which is an amazing institution. At the end of the senior year, all the young men who are Catholics get invited to a daylong retreat at the college. The purpose of the retreat is to invite them to consider joining the Christian Brothers religious order and becoming an educator. The retreat was voluntary, but turning down the invitation simply wasn't done. I was willing to go, but I had no intention of joining anything.

By this point in my life, I had wrestled with matters of faith enough to know that I could not accept everything the Church taught—to the consternation of some of my conservative Catholic friends. Still, I did have faith, and I considered myself a fairly spiritual person. But what I did not have was much patience for church services, which, to be honest, usually bored me to tears. So I can't say that I was looking forward to the day, which was to culminate with a Mass attended by all the Brothers and all the students.

For most of the event, we simply hung out in the residence area, getting to know all the Christian Brothers. I found myself playing blackjack with several of them, and I remember that I really cleaned up. The day was pleasant enough but essentially unremarkable.

And then it came time for the Mass.

I cannot explain what happened next. All I know is that there we were, all of us in a chapel, gathered in a spirit of love and affection and fellowship, when without warning I began experiencing an emotion that I can barely describe. It was something like euphoria, although that word doesn't quite do it justice. In a flash, suddenly I was feeling every soul in the room, every beating heart, every good wish, every kind thought, every loving emotion, all of it as it flowed through me and through each of us. The feeling was completely unexpected and hit me upside the head like a brickbat. I can't say what triggered it. One moment I was standing there, bored, as usual, with the Mass, of which I had seen many. The next moment I was caught up in a spiritual glow that was almost, but not quite, visible, and certainly was palpable. It took my breath away, and practically lifted me off my feet.

All my life I'd been taught about the Holy Trinity. When I was young the custom was to refer to that third incarnation as "The Holy Ghost." By the time I was in high school, more often you heard it referred to as the "Holy Spirit." My only concept of it was that it supposedly had descended on the Disciples who'd gathered after the Crucifixion of Christ. I had no idea what that supposed descent meant.

Until that moment. No, I heard no rush of wind. There were no tongues of fire. But I swear to you, I *knew*. Whatever those disciples had felt as described in the New Testament, I experienced it, or something very much like it, that day.

It did not last long. But to this day, I can recall the feeling, and it has never lost its power. My eyes are filling with tears as I type this.

I say it was a miracle. The faithful may agree. But I said earlier that I would not foist religion on you. You don't have to believe that the Holy Spirit descended if that conflicts with your world view. I do ask you to accept my words at face value, though, that something extraordinary did happen. The literature is filled with examples of humans making heart-to-heart connections. They've even been known to reach out across vast distances to do so— and here we were, all gathered in one small place. Maybe what happened was simply another, more intense manifestation of Jung's collective unconscious. Or, if it makes you feel better to call it things like "extreme empathy" or "extreme introspection," I will not argue with you. What's most important in terms of this narrative is not the cause, but the effects that this had on me.

And here it is: The event completely changed my life philosophy and gave me a new direction. I resolved from that moment forward to have a goal of adding only positive energy to the universe, and to be, wherever possible, an inspiration to people, not a drag on their spirits.

Look, I claim to be better than absolutely nobody. I'm a flawed being—more flawed than most, I'd say. I have not always achieved that goal, and there are periods of my life where my actions strayed fairly far from it. But even so, I've never turned my back on those ideals. I have always held them in mind, and I consider myself to be at my best when I am adding positive vibes to a situation where someone else might react with darker emotions. As the philosophy translates to a career as a TV news director, I have tried to inspire those working with me to set high standards and to remember why we do what we do, which is, ultimately, to benefit people and be a force for good. I don't know if I would have been the same person with the same philosophy and direction had this event not taken place.

Here's one thing the experience did *not* do. Clearly what it did not do was to arm me with an impenetrable shield against despair—submission to which the Church teaches is one of the greatest mortal sins. And yet, somehow I survived it all. Could it be that this one moment of exposure to what I choose to call The Holy Spirit really did make the difference in who I became?

Skeptics, no doubt, will argue that I'm just deluding myself in thinking that anything "miraculous" took place. Call it what you want. But here's the thing. Whatever happened, it *did* guide me. I *did* become a more spiritual being. I *did* survive against long odds. These events *did* inspire me and that inspiration *did* last a lifetime. I've never lost the thought that my life was supposed to mean something. I have dedicated myself from that moment to trying to make a positive difference. The path I ultimately chose was not religious in nature (I was tempted to join the order, but I knew celibacy was not for me). Instead I devoted myself to journalism. I know I've been involved in news stories that have made a positive impact on the world. I also know, through the many, many people who've contacted me since news of my cancer broke, that over the course of my life I have served as an inspiration to at least some of those I've mentored over the years, who in turn have dedicated themselves at least in part to similar ideals.

And *that* is the second miracle—not the long odds that caused me to survive that which arguably should not have been survived, but rather the newly inspired and redirected life that followed.

When something like this happens to you, you can't help but believe that it did so "for a reason" and that your life therefore "is supposed to mean something." Everyone to whom I've told the story of my suicide attempt certainly has had that reaction, which they tend to express with words like this: "Clearly, God had a purpose in mind for you."

But I said earlier that you would not require religious convictions to learn something from this story. Now, as the end of my life approaches, I cannot swear to you that I came out of my 1975-1976 experiences having been "given" a purpose. But I can swear that I did emerge with a renewed *sense* of purpose. I chose that purpose myself. Yes, I did promise myself and my God that I would not waste the second chance I'd been given. But you do not have to believe in God to acknowledge that I made a promise, or to accept my testimony that, having done so, I spent my life trying to keep my eye on the ball and work toward fulfilling that promise. Sharing this story with you about how I nearly threw away that life, but didn't, and then spent the rest of my days embracing a newfound sense of purpose and direction, is part of that fulfillment. I did it. *Anyone* can.

For many decades now, I have never failed to wake up in the morning and greet the sunrise without a sense of wonder, surprise, and gratitude. Now that I know my time is nearly up, many people have been astounded at my high spirits and positive attitude. What they don't realize is that I have considered every single moment since that fateful day in 1976 to have been bonus play, and I still do. Every new day behind me was a new gift. Every day to come will be one as well, bestowed on a person who was, and is, in no way deserving of it.

It staggers the mind to think of everything I would have given up had I died in 1976. I have had some wonderful relatives and have won some amazing friends. I've loved deeply, and have been loved. I met the love of my life, my wonderful wife Deborah, who bestowed on me the amazing gift of sharing her *entire life* with me; we are still together, and every day I look at her with a new sense of amazement. When I think of the laughter, and the passion, and The Ventures and Electric Light Orchestra and all the rock bands and others genres of music I learned to love, and Robert Heinlein, and *2001: A Space Odyssey* and *Star Trek*, and real-life space exploration, and Quarter Pounders with Cheese, and little kitty people, and ski trips, and Arizona sunsets, and Florida thunderstorms and the hiss of soft waves on the beach at night, and summer evening cicadas in Tennessee, and Memphis in May, and driving cross country in my Mustang, and all the people I've known and been inspired by and perhaps have inspired in return—well, the list goes on and on and on. Every item on it was special and I nearly threw out every one.

*But I didn't.*

Perhaps you are now experiencing a dark moment that is causing you to consider doing what I nearly did, and ending it all. Or maybe you're just going through a bleak period, and are having a hard time finding any joy in your life. In either case, I want you to pause for a moment, and consider this fact: If you define a miracle as an event that happens against long odds and which benefits someone, then *you* are a miracle. Yes, *you personally.*

Let me explain. The sperm that conceived you was probably one of about 40,000,000 that were competing for the honor at that moment. The egg was probably about one in 1,500,000. When the one particular sperm and the one particular egg that became you started their day, the odds of them linking up were about 2 in a hundred trillion. And that's only looking at that *one day*; the odds decrease even further over the lifetime of the parents. Now add in two sets of grandparents. The odds that the specific 3 sperm and the specific 3 eggs that came together to contribute to the youness of you would actually do so now fall to about five in a tredecillion. The latter is $10^{42}$—ten to the forty-second power, or a 1 with 42 zeroes after it. To put that number into perspective for you, the number of stars in the observable universe is believed to be about $10^{29}$. In other words, you are more unique than any star in existence—by a factor of 10,000,000,000,000!

And those odds are just from having gone back two

generations. Start going back further than that, and odds of all the specific eggs and all the specific sperm coming together in such a way as to be responsible for you being here become so vanishingly small as to amount to—well, here's that word again: a miracle. To the faithful, that's exactly what it was, an act of God. But you don't have to be religious to stand in awe of it and to value it.

And those are only the *genetic* odds. When you look at everything else that had to happen for your parents to meet and conceive you, it blows the mind. Again, here's another example from my past. My father commanded a tank platoon on Saipan, yet managed to survive the deadly battle of Death Valley. But that wasn't his closest call. According to the story he told, one day his platoon was out on maneuvers when one of his tanks hit a 500 pound aerial bomb that the Japanese defenders had buried as a mine. The explosion was powerful enough to send the 17-ton tank flying into the air and bring it down on its turret, killing everyone instantly. At this point, as my father told it, he had three choices: continue with the patrol, turn around, or stop right there. He chose the latter, ordering a dismount and calling for Army engineers to come sweep the field. A short time later, one of them found the detonator of a 500 pound aerial bomb protruding from the sand six inches in front of my father's left tank tread. Any other decision, or even a split-second delay in making the one he had, would have resulted in his death, and then I wouldn't be here, either. Nor would the children of the other three members of his tank crew. Nor would my four nieces and three nephews. Or the children they'll have some day. And so on.

So you see, each of us really is incredibly special. It's something to think about, especially on those days that seem very dark. And we all have them, because that is the nature of human existence. I swear to you by all that is holy—or, if you're not into that, by all that is *good*—that each of us will have a walk through the valley of the shadow of death, because it is only through such a journey that we can understand what it means to have joy. But we are not meant to live in that valley. If you keep moving forward, you will emerge from the shadows. Trust me. If I can do it, I promise you that anyone can.

Having made a promise to keep moving forward, by sometime in my mid-20's I had put depression behind me and it never troubled me again. Now, given what I have been through and am yet to go through, I don't understand people who wring their hands about the meaning of life. Life is not a question. It is the answer! The meaning of life is *life*! Glorious, incredible, miraculous *life*—the simple fact of existing, with self-awareness, the ability to sense our surroundings, and the capacity to care for one another—and, on the rarest of occasions, to merge our souls with another being. Life is the gift that makes all other gifts possible.

The universe cannot give meaning to life. In fact, it's the other way around: *Life gives meaning to the universe.* Without us here observe it, and experience it, and celebrate it, it would be exactly as if the universe did not exist at all.

So, your life has meaning. It does not, however, come pre-stamped with a *purpose*. You have to decide that for yourself. The freedom to make such a choice also is a great gift.

My time is nearly up. Yours will be too, although hopefully for you that day still lies way down the road. I don't know about you, but if I have a choice, I don't plan to lie around in the afterlife sitting on a cloud and scratching my butt. I want back in the game. Show me where I can get a ticket. This ride has its bumps, but man, is it fun. I want to go again.

So, this is my gift to you, and I hope you will accept it, embrace it, and share it with others that might benefit from reading these words. Life is more wonderful than you can possibly imagine. And we are connected to our fellow humans in ways that aren't always immediately apparent. If you open your eyes and ears and heart to all the possibilities, your life can be amazingly rich. I hope my words will help inspire you to do that, to make every moment count, and to help others do the same.

May all your dreams be wondrous. And may your life exceed them.

# APPENDIX A: SUPPORTING
# DOCUMENTATION

## 2001 Fully-refundable Travel Receipt Excerpt

From: Southwest Airlines [no-reply@mail.southwest.com]
Sent: Tuesday, September 04, 2001 3:13 PM
To: Carr, Forrest
Subject: Ticketless Confirmation

Thank you for purchasing Southwest Airlines
Ticketless Travel. For questions or changes
concerning your reservation, call 1-800-I-FLY-SWA
(1-800-435-9792).

*************** RECEIPT AND ITINERARY
***********

Southwest Airlines Ticketless Travel
Non Transferable. Positive Identification Required.
If not checking luggage, simply proceed to your
departure gate.

Receipt and Itinerary as of 09/04/01 02:12PM

\* \* \* \* \* \* \* \* \* \* \* \* \* \* \*
Confirmation Number: MUBA6P
Confirmation Date: 09/04/01
\* \* \* \* \* \* \* \* \* \* \* \* \* \* \*

Received: FORREST

Passenger(s):
CARR/FORREST 526-2771673931-2

Itinerary:
Wednesday, September 12 - TAMPA INTL to
NASHVILLE TN2570Flight 797 Y
Depart TAMPA INTL at 11:20AM and
Arrive NASHVILLE TN at 12:05PM

Friday, September 14 - NASHVILLE TN to TAMPA
INTL2570Flight 1398 Y
Depart NASHVILLE TN at 07:40PM and
Arrive TAMPA INTL at 10:25PM

\*\*\*\*\*\*\*\*\*\*\*\*\*\*\*\*\*\*\*\*\* COST \*\*\*\*\*\*\*\*\*\*\*\*\*\*\*\*\*\*\*\*\*

Total for 1 Passenger(s)
AIR: ...........$277.20
TAX: ...........$26.30
PFC: ...........$6.00

_____

Total Fare: $309.50

\*\*\*\*\*\*\*\*\*\*\*\*\*\*\*       PAYMENT       SUMMARY
\*\*\*\*\*\*\*\*\*\*\*\*\*\*\*\*\*

Current payment(s)
04SEP2001 AMER EXPRESS xxxxxxxxxxx4002 Ref 526-

2771673931-2 $309.50

Total Payments: $309.50

\*\*\*\*\*\*\*\*            REFUND            INFORMATION
\*\*\*\*\*\*\*\*\*\*\*\*\*\*\*\*\*\*

Any change to this itinerary may result in a
fare increase. If you do not travel on this itinerary,
you may qualify for a refund or an exchange. To make
application for a refund of any unused air fare,
please write:

Southwest Airlines Refunds Department
6RF, P.O. Box 36611,
Dallas, TX 75235-1611.

Refund requests must include your confirmation number,
date of travel and flight number, and all credit card
billing information including the amount and purchase
reference numbers.

This is a post only mailing from Southwest Airlines
regarding your flight confirmation.

Please do not attempt to respond to this message.

## 2008 Email with a Very Surprised Acquaintance

From: [NAME REDACTED]
Sent: Thursday, November 20, 2008 11:01 AM
To: Forrest Carr
Subject: What the hell!

You've been News Director across the street since September and I'm just finding out you're here?!?!?!
Boy I really am out of the news loop.
[NAME AND TITLE REDACTED]
KOB-TV

From: Forrest Carr
Sent: Thursday, November 20, 2008 11:20 AM
To: [NAME REDACTED]
Subject: RE: What the hell!

You have GOT to be kidding me. I swear to God, your name popped into my head this morning as I was getting ready for work, for no reason whatsoever, and I spent several minutes wondering where you were these days and what you were up to. I kid you not. We have to do lunch. Immediately. I'm booked for the rest of this week but next week is way open through Wednesday. Do you have a hole in your schedule?
FC

Forrest Carr
News Director
KRQE/KASA
13 Broadcast Plaza SW
Albuquerque, NM 87104

-------------------------------------------------------------------------
--------

**Excerpt from My Resignation Announcement, posted on Facebook March 13, 2013:**

"By now many of you have heard the rumors about my impending departure from KGUN9 News. I want to take a moment to let my friends and colleagues know what is going on with me, and what I see ahead for the next phase of my life.

"I'm now in my 34th year as a TV news professional, and my 24th as a TV news manager. This profession is incredibly demanding, and the management side of it is more so. I have not routinely worked an 8-hour day since 1989. As news director, you can leave the office, but you're never really off duty. Even a weekend trip -- scheduled on your nominal 'days off' -- takes careful coordination, and can't happen during a 'sweeps' month. The business and competitive pressures are constant -- and in today's Internet and social media age, the stress has never been higher. The job tries its best to consume every waking moment, and there are days and even weeks where it not only succeeds, but cuts into what would have been and should have been non-waking moments, too. It is a high pressure, high stress, high turnover gig. Very few of my colleagues who were TV news directors when I became one in 1997 are still working in that same capacity today. The news industry trade magazines, web sites and newsletters are filled with example after example of news directors leaving after only two years or less on the job, having originally replaced someone who also worked for two years or so, and so on.

"There are things I'd like to accomplish in life that I just haven't found the time to do. The occasional deaths of colleagues about my age serve as a reminder that it's not safe to wait until retirement to do the things you want to do; you may not make it. You may not even get close.

"So, last week I decided to resign my position. My last official day is Friday of next week.

"I'm by no means the first TV news director to take this step.

"What lies ahead? First, I plan to take a long road trip and reconnect with some friends, some of whom I haven't seen in quite a while. After that, I will work on my 'bucket list' project, which will be to finish up two novels, possibly write a third that I'm carrying around in my head, and make a concerted effort to get them published. I don't know if I have what it takes to succeed in such an endeavor, but I'm going to find out, once and for all."

FORREST CARR

# APPENDIX B: EVOLUTION VS. INTELLIGENT DESIGN—DO WE HAVE A WINNER?

*Some scientists now say that life on earth may have begun a billion years earlier than they'd originally thought. But the breakthrough finding still leaves evolutionary science empty handed in answering two key questions: How did life start? And why, despite the conditions for life on earth being so perfect, did it only happen once, and then never again?*

You gotta love Charles Darwin. Ever since he put forth a theory in the 19th century that all life on Earth is descended from a common ancestor—yes, he's saying you are great-great-great-whatever-grandson or granddaughter to an amoeba or something like it—organized religion has had its figurative shorts in a bunch. First, the outraged faithful tried to ban the teaching of evolution in schools. The Scopes "Monkey Trial" threw a major wrench into those efforts, but Darwin haters haven't given up. More recently, believers came up with a new tactic to fight back against the science of evolution: "Intelligent Design." This is the idea that life is too complex to be explained by a process so undirected as evolution, and therefore must involve the work of an intelligence. ID authors normally don't name the Designer. But if the Designer walks like a duck—well, you get the idea. Given that many of the most prominent proponents of ID began life as creationists, you don't have to look hard to see what they're up to. ID is their way of inserting God back into the classroom—and, by extension, back into science.

Every now and then a controversy erupts when an institution of learning refuses to let the ID folks inject their beliefs where they don't belong. A 2013 uproar involving Ball State University is typical. That year it banned the teaching of Intelligent Design in science classes, after someone complained about a physics professor who argued that nature shows evidence of the concept in action. Four state legislators rushed to his rescue, going to battle with the university president in the name of "academic freedom." But these politicians wear their motives on their sleeves. One of them, according to news reports, had tried previously to pass legislation requiring the teaching of Creationism—the belief that God created the world more less as described in the Bible—in school.

Speaking personally, I have no problem believing that if there is a God, that he might choose to accomplish His works through the very laws of nature that He created. If so, it stands to reason that someday man should be able to understand those principles. So let's examine the science of evolution. Does it explain everything?

In a word, no. Nor does it claim to. But what evolution has done is to lay out many incontrovertible facts for us that shed light on how the life process works. Among them is the fact that life evolves—in other words, it changes form over time. Another is that life has existed on earth for billions of years, and most definitely was *not* created over the course of a six-day workweek just a few thousand years ago. These are observed certainties, as absolutely and concretely factual as this morning's sunrise, and equally as impossible to explain away. Religious zealots who refuse to accept this put themselves into the same class as someone who might stubbornly cling to the notion that the earth is flat, thereby zeroing themselves out of the conversation; it's impossible to have a rational discussion with someone who is not open to the actual facts.

Despite their roots in creationism, and despite their goal of discrediting evolutionary theory, ID proponents typically do not claim out loud the world was created in a week. That's good, because there's a lot to talk about—and therefore argue about—for anyone who is willing to embrace the reality of the facts uncovered so far. There are still plenty of blanks to be filled in. Not every aspect of the evolutionary process is fully understood. Scientists are still very busy looking for new facts, exploring new avenues, and forming and testing new hypotheses. That's how the discipline of science—and there's that word again, *science*—works. The final word on the study of evolution has not been written. Far from it. It may never be.

One principle of evolution that sends the faithful through the roof is that the process has no purpose or plan. The question, "Where are we going with all this, and why?" has no scientific answer. Nor does evolution address the question of how life, and the universe itself, came to be in the first place. Evolutionary science is a set of observations in need of an explanation.

Intelligent Design is the opposite. It's an explanation in need of an observation. Intelligent Design teaches that evolution can't explain why we're here. It then concludes that God—or something that looks and sounds very much like God—must be responsible. That conclusion sounds reasonable and obvious to the faithful. But it does not derive *scientifically* from a study of the available facts. ID offers no hypotheses that can be tested. Its key conclusion, that some kind of intelligence exists that is responsible for designing life—requires a leap of faith to believe. This makes ID a religion, not a science.

There's nothing wrong with that. But religion does not

have a place in any science class. Such classes are, by definition, reserved for the study of *science*. Religion is taught down the hall or a couple of buildings over, under the auspices of a different department.

Yet evolutionary scientists should pay attention to what ID advocates are saying anyway. ID's answers may fall short scientifically, but the *questions* it asks are perfectly valid. That is why this passionate argument will not go away.

Many processes are involved in the morphing of simple life forms into complex ones, and the divergence of existing species into new ones. At the heart of the process is genetic mutation—the general idea being that random changes occur every so often in individual genetic material, the code that defines the organism. As the theory goes, "good" mutations (bad ones are lethal) give rise to beneficial new characteristics and behaviors that favor survival and reproduction of the organism. This leads to offspring that are better suited to thrive, who then pass the mutation down, and there you go—natural selection, or "survival of the fittest" as it's sometimes called.

But this theory requires us to believe that life, in all its glorious complexity, essentially is the product of a series of random events. According to current evolutionary theory, ultimately we're all just a collection of organic chemicals that somehow, over the eons, got lucky and managed to organize, crawl out of the ooze, and eventually become self aware, if somewhat confused.

It is even theoretically possible for random chance to pull off such a seemingly miraculous accomplishment?

There's an old saying in the study of chance and probability that if you were to put an infinite number of monkeys in an infinitely large room and have them bang away on an infinite set of keyboards for an infinite amount of time, they'd produce every book that's ever been written or ever will be written. This may be true in a mathematical sense, but it's misleading bunk anyway. First, you'd have to have an infinity of time to work with. And even then, the resulting random productions of something that look intelligible would be completely lost in the noise, so buried in an infinitely huge mound of gibberish as to be undetectable and unusable. Life on earth is not noise. But even more to the point, no infinite amount of time has transpired between the beginning of life and the present day in which to produce the biological masterpieces we see before us. In geological terms, 3.8 billion years is not exactly a blink of an eye, but nor is it anywhere near an infinity of time. Plants and animals populating the earth today are incredibly complex, to the point where not every aspect of how they function is understood even now. If these organisms were machines, we'd call them the products of amazing, jaw-dropping, breathtaking genius. In a sense, they *are* machines—biological ones.

This is the place where ID adherents depart from the evolutionists. They scoff at the notion that such seemingly ingenious complexity could possibly be the product of random chance.

They have a point.

As just one example, take the human visual system, beginning with the eye. Here we have a small round sphere of opaque tissue, into which a hole covered by *transparent* tissue has been placed to allow the introduction of light. There is a muscular mechanism to bend this lens in such a way as to focus the light into an image. The interior of the sphere is filled with transparent liquid, to allow the light to pass through and strike a wall of tissue at the rear, where the image then forms. This receiving tissue contains receptors that translate the light data into nerve impulses. A nerve transmits these impulses to the visual cortex in the human brain, which is then able to reinterpret this data into an image. Any one of the features and sub-systems described above would be amazing enough by itself. The assembled mechanism is fantastically astonishing beyond words. The eye even comes in nifty designer colors. All this is the product of *random chance?* It beggars the imagination.

Still, let's not be hasty. Why don't we try a little experiment and see if we can determine how long it would take to construct a given genetic pattern by random chance alone.

Not to get too technical—but very roughly speaking, the human genome is made up of a linear sequence of codes in the form of specific organic compound base pairs, each of which can have one of four values. Genomes are passed down to the next generation exclusively through sex cells. So for a mutation to occur and survive, it has to happen within a sex cell prior to or during reproduction.

Let's take a hypothetical species with a genome measuring 100 base pairs long. In other words, our organism is defined by a 100-character word, written in a language containing only four letters. For the purpose of our experiment, we're looking for a specific word that will encode the precise qualities and capabilities we're looking for. And let's be generous and say that our test species reproduces once an hour, and has current stable population of five billion, with births just keeping pace with deaths. Now, let's start with the first letter of our word. To achieve a 100% probability of getting the correct choice by random chance, we'd have to roll our die (in this case, a specially-designed one containing just four letter choices) four times. Now let's move on to the next position. To be sure of getting that one right also requires four rolls of the die. But to reach a 100% probability of getting it right *at the same time the one next to it is correct* requires us to roll *two* dice, and to toss them 4 x 4 times—4 to the second power, sixteen rolls in all. In other words, with sixteen tosses you can achieve a 100% probability that at least one of those tosses will produce the specific two-letter combination desired. However, to be sure of getting the *entire* sequence exactly as you want it by random chance alone would require us to roll a hundred dice in each throw, one for each character position, and do it $4^{100}$ times—which works out to 1.6 novemdecillion rolls. A novemdecillion is a 1 followed by 60 zeros.

And remember, we're allowing ourselves 5 billion throws an hour. That may seem like a lot, but to go through every combination at that rate in order to hit that 100% probability of success, we'd have work at it for 36 quattuordecillion years. A quattuordecillion is $10^{45}$—a one with 45 zeroes.

Of course, you could get lucky and hit your precise combination on the very first roll. You'd need lots and *lots* of luck. Your odds of hitting the right combination on any given toss would be 1 in 1.6 novemdecillion. Or, put another way the odds of success in one roll would be:

1                                                                                    in
1,600,000,000,000,000,000,000,000,000,000,000,000,000,00
0,000,000,000,000,000,000.

Now, admittedly, our test is very simplified compared to real life. For one, at any given time the natural mutation process is likely to affect only a small number of the base pairs, if any, and certainly not all of them at once. In that sense, our experiment speeded things up considerably. We cut out the natural selection process, which decides whether a given mutation will survive or thrive. And we started our word at the desired length and kept it there, rather than allowing it to grow additional character positions, which would have changed the odds even further.

But now think about this. The genome for our hypothetical test organism was only 100 base pairs long. The smallest genomes we actually know about, such as those found in viruses and bacteria, are at least 2,000 times *larger*. The human genome is 31 *million* times larger—3.1 billion base pairs in all. To be assured of coming up with any one particular base pair sequence in a genome that large would require 4 to the 3.1 billionth power throws, using 3.1 billion dice at a time! When I try to make my calculator spit out that number, it gives me a message that says "OFLO," which I take to mean, "Oh, for the love of —" When I try it on any of several web-based applications I found online, the result is "Infinity." In fact, I get that same result for any power over about *500*. Or, putting it another way, your odds of getting it right on any given toss would be 1 in $4^{3,100,000,000}$ (a percentage that also makes my HP 20s Scientific Calculator's eyes cross). And by the way, our human reproductive cycle takes considerably longer than one hour for a generation.

And yet we've managed to get here in just 4 billion years. To me, that is a very strong argument against the idea that random chance alone is responsible for the existence of life on earth in all its current complexity.

So let's say, hypothetically and just for grins, that some *other* kind of force or principle is at work. If chance didn't do it, does that mean God did?

No. The data for such a conclusion are not at hand. Not yet, anyway.

There is, however, another huge hole in what evolution can explain. One of the basic tenets of modern physics is that the laws of the universe are the same everywhere. For instance, our sun is not unique, and it functions along the same lines as other stars in our galaxy, and also stars in *other* galaxies for as far out as we can see.

Similarly, chemical processes are universal in nature. To use a more localized example, lightning strikes a tree, which bursts into flame. It's not the first time a tree has burned, nor will it be the last. The fire may die out, but the chemical laws that created it remain. The next time the conditions are right, fire will be seen again.

Nature doesn't seem to do anything just once. Yet, when it comes to life on earth, that's exactly what appears to have happened. Sometime around 3.8 billion years ago, the conditions for life were right. Life therefore erupted. *Yet it's never happened again.* Scientists generally agree that every organism on earth belongs to the same "tree of life," having descended from a one single-celled life form of some sort that formed billions of years ago. Whether that ancestor cell was the first to arise from the lifeless soup of organic chemicals that gave it birth, we don't know. Perhaps other trees of life emerged and then died out, leaving only the one that led to all life on earth as we now know it.

But in all of the billions of years since our ancestor cell took root, there has not been another single instance of life creation that we know of. Why not? Life seems to have erupted the moment conditions were right, which happened very soon after the planet cooled. Conditions for life on earth certainly seem to be pretty favorable now. So why has there never been another life-forming "Genesis" in all the billions of years since the one that led to us? What process created life, and then went dormant? Such one-time, unique events are *not* how nature is supposed to work.

Doesn't it say something that even though we have been able to duplicate the conditions of primordial earth in the lab, those experiments have *not* led to the creation of life? Where did that original life spark come from? It's exactly as if the lightning-sparked fire in the analogy above erupted one time, but no new fires ever broke out after that in any other place, even though the conditions for both lightning and fire remained exactly the same, or even better.

And while we're raising questions—what evolutionary survival-favoring function do tears serve? Why do we grieve when we lose a loved one? Why do we laugh when amused? Why do cats purr? Why do dogs wag their tails? In what genetic mutations are such behaviors rooted?

In science, if an hypothesis doesn't satisfactorily explain all the known facts, then it doesn't fit. Conversely, even hypotheses that do fit the facts sometimes have to be rejected in favor of new ones that explain the facts better.

And quite often, the discovery of new facts completely shatters old notions. History shows that scientists sometimes vigorously resist such breakthroughs when they first occur. Darwin's evolutionary theory itself is an example of that. Now ID proponents cry out for evolutionary scientists to do better. They're not wrong to do so. Scientists should listen.

Proposition (an intriguing idea yet to be proved): Something is going on with genetic mutation and the forming of organs and organisms *other* than just random chance combined with natural selection. What is it? How does it work? Scientists would do well to keep digging. And they are doing so, following the leads wherever the day takes them.

Intelligent Design proponents should take fair warning, however, that even if some other force, agent, or principle ultimately is found to be at work, it doesn't mean that force, agent, or principle "must" be a designer, "must" be intelligent, or "must" be God or even an entity of any kind. It's tempting to say that divine intervention must be responsible for anything that science can't immediately explain. And indeed, there is a long history of scientists themselves chalking up stubborn mysteries to the Almighty. No less that the great Sir Isaac Newton himself, in his groundbreaking work *Philosophiae Naturalis Principia Mathematica*, attributed some planetary motions he couldn't quite explain to the guiding hand of God. Later, physicist Pierre Laplace used better calculations to connect all the dots, and was able to explain the motions without referencing God. Napoleon Bonaparte famously asked Laplace why he left God out. "I had no need of that hypothesis," Laplace is reputed to have said. This anecdote contributed to the public's notion that science essentially is godless.

Really, it's not true. Science is not the enemy of religion. Nor does the reverse have to be true. If you are religious, there is nothing blasphemous in the idea that

117

God might choose to work within the rules of the physical laws He created. Scientific discoveries lead us toward the creator—if there is one—not away. If you're not a believer, then science itself may someday solve enough of the universe's mysteries to convince you. Maybe not. In any case, science will not be complete until it can answer, with scientific rigor, the questions the faithful have already found their own way to resolve.

NOTES

1 http://www.nytimes.com/1995/07/18/science/
lost-japanese-sub-with-2-tons-of-axis-gold-found-on-
floor-of-atlantic.html

2 http://www-t.nationalgeographic.com/
ngm/9910/hilights.html#g

3 http://www.cnn.com/2013/11/30/world/europe/
scotland-helicopter-crash/

4 http://www.nydailynews.com/news/national/violent-
teen-mob-attacks-shoppers-workers-tenn-grocery-store-
video-article-1.1931987

5 http://www.theguardian.com/world/2015/mar/18/
kazakhstan-sleeping-village-mystery

6 https://archive.org/details/phantasmsoflivin02gurniala

7 http://www.rtdna.org/article/
rtdna_september_11_reflections#.VThRZpOrGzk

8  http://www.amazon.com/The-
Parapsychology-Revolution-Anthology-Paranormal/
dp/1585426164

9 http://amasci.com/weird/vindac.html

10 http://www2.ucsc.edu/dreams/Library/fmid9.html

11 http://www.amazon.com/The-Dimensions-Dreams-
Function-Interpretation/dp/1843100681

12  http://www.thefreedictionary.com/miracle

# ABOUT THE AUTHOR

Forrest Carr is a novelist, blogger and former radio talk show host and journalist who spent 33 years in the television news industry, serving as a news director in the Tampa, Fort Myers, Albuquerque, and Tucson television markets. Carr has received or shared credit in more than 90 professional awards, including a Suncoast Regional Emmy and two regional Edward R. Murrow awards for investigative reporting, and is a co-author of *Broadcast News Handbook*, a college textbook published by McGraw-Hill, now in its fifth edition. Carr is author of the novel *Messages,* a "buddy journalist" crime story that shows how TV news evolved into its current state; *A Journal of the Crazy Year*, a prophetic zombie-genre post-apocalyptic tale inspired by an actual disease; and *The Dark,* a sci-fi novel about the most ambitious space voyage in human history, what happens at the end of it, and what that says about mankind's relationship with God. Carr is a long-time fan of old school science fiction, particularly the works of Robert Heinlein. He resides with his wife Deborah and their two cats Ellis and Mina, a.k.a. Butthead 1 and Butthead Also, in Tucson, Arizona. He invites readers to reach him through his author page on Facebook or by way of his website, www.forrestcarr.com.

www.ingramcontent.com/pod-product-compliance
Lightning Source LLC
Chambersburg PA
CBHW060516030426
42337CB00015B/1912